W9-AVT-324

CliffsNotes™

Understanding Life Insurance

By Bart Astor

IN THIS BOOK

- Make sense of the different types of life insurance
- Determine which type of life insurance is best for you
- Assess what your life is worth
- Understand the role of life insurance in estate planning
- Choose a company, policy, and agent that match your needs
- Reinforce what you learn with CliffsNotes Review
- Find more life insurance information in CliffsNotes Resource Center and online at www.cliffsnotes.com

IDG Books Worldwide, Inc.
An International Data Group Company

Foster City, CA • Chicago, IL • Indianapolis, IN • New York, NY

IDG BOOKS WORLDWIDE

About the Author

Bart Astor, a freelance writer based in Virginia, is the author of six books and numerous articles that have appeared in national magazines. His previous book, *Baby Boomers Guide to Caring for Aging Parents*, has been featured on several radio and television talk shows, including ABC's *Good Morning America*, *Fox Morning News*, and National Public Radio's *Marketplace*. Mr. Astor was also series editor and coauthor of four books on college admission and financial aid, a contributing author and editor for various college guides, and publisher of a national newsletter on college planning.

Publisher's Acknowledgments

Editorial

Project Editors: Christine Meloy Beck, Pamela Mourouzis

Acquisitions Editors: Mark Butler, Karen Hansen

Senior Copy Editor: Tamara Castleman

Technical Reviewers: George W. Bailey, Carol A. Mitchell

Production

Indexer: York Production Services

Proofreader: York Production Services

IDG Books Indianapolis Production Department

CliffsNotes™ Understanding Life Insurance

Published by

IDG Books Worldwide, Inc.

An International Data Group Company

919 E. Hillsdale Blvd.

Suite 400

Foster City, CA 94404

www.idgbooks.com (IDG Books Worldwide Web site)

www.cliffsnotes.com (CliffsNotes Web site)

Distributed in the United States by IDG Books Worldwide, Inc.

Distributed by CDG Books Canada Inc. for Canada; by Transworld Publishers Limited in the United Kingdom; by IDG Norge Books for Norway; by IDG Sweden Books for Sweden; by IDG Books Australia Publishing Corporation Pty. Ltd. for Australia and New Zealand; by TransQuest Publishers Pte Ltd. for Singapore, Malaysia, Thailand, Indonesia, and Hong Kong; by Gotop Information Inc. for Taiwan; by ICG Muse, Inc. for Japan; by Norma Comunicaciones S.A. for Colombia; by Intersoft for South Africa; by Eyrolles for France; by International Thomson Publishing for Germany, Austria and Switzerland; by Distribuidora Cuspide for Argentina; by Livraria Cultura for Brazil; by Ediciones ZETA S.C.R. Ltda. for Peru; by WS Computer Publishing Corporation, Inc., for the Philippines; by Contemporanea de Ediciones for Venezuela; by Express Computer Distributors for the Caribbean and West Indies; by Micronesia Media Distributor, Inc. for Micronesia; by Grupo Editorial Norma S.A. for Guatemala; by Chips Computadoras S.A. de C.V. for Mexico; by Editorial Norma de Panama S.A. for Panama; by American Bookshops for Finland. Authorized Sales Agent: Anthony Rudkin Associates for the Middle East and North Africa.

For general information on IDG Books Worldwide's books in the U.S., please call our Consumer Customer Service department at **800-762-2974**. For reseller information, including discounts and premium sales, please call our Reseller Customer Service department at **800-434-3422**.

For information on where to purchase IDG Books Worldwide's books outside the U.S., please contact our International Sales department at 317-596-5530 or fax **317-596-5692**.

For consumer information on foreign language translations, please contact our Customer Service department at **1-800-434-3422**, fax **317-596-5692**, or e-mail rights@idgbooks.com.

For information on licensing foreign or domestic rights, please phone **+1-650-655-3109**.

For sales inquiries and special prices for bulk quantities, please contact our Sales department at 650-655-3200 or write to the address above.

For information on using IDG Books Worldwide's books in the classroom or for ordering examination copies, please contact our Educational Sales department at **800-434-2086** or fax **317-596-5499**.

For press review copies, author interviews, or other publicity information, please contact our Public Relations department at **650-655-3000** or fax **650-655-3299**.

For authorization to photocopy items for corporate, personal, or educational use, please contact Copyright Clearance Center, 222 Rosewood Drive, Danvers, MA 01923, or fax **978-750-4470**.

Table of Contents

INTRODUCTION

Life insurance is a unique product. Like other insurance products, its primary purpose is to protect against loss. But unlike other kinds of insurance products, life insurance isn't for you; it's for your survivors. Life insurance has no uncertainties; if you're covered by a life insurance policy — and the company holding the policy has the resources to pay — you can pretty much bet that someday your survivors *will* receive a benefit. Knowing how much life insurance coverage to buy isn't an easy decision; evaluating a car or a house is fairly simple, but how do you figure the value of your life?

Why Do You Need This Book?

Can you answer yes to any of these questions?

- Do you need to learn about life insurance fast?
- Do you not have time to read 500 pages on life insurance?
- Do you need to find out about the different types of life insurance?
- Do you need to find an insurance company, an insurance agent, and a specific policy?

If so, then CliffsNotes *Understanding Life Insurance* is for you!

How to Use This Book

This book discusses key things you need to know to make informed decisions about life insurance.

You can read this book straight through or just look for the information you need. You can find information on a particular topic in a number of ways: You can search the index in the back of the book, locate your topic in the Table of Contents, or read the In This Chapter list in each chapter. To reinforce your learning, check out the Review and the Resource Center at the back of the book. To help you find important information in the book, look for the following icons in the text:

This icon points out something worth keeping in mind.

This icon clues you in to helpful hints and advice.

This icon alerts you to something dangerous or to avoid.

Don't Miss Our Web Site

Keep up with the changing world of insurance by visiting the CliffsNotes Web site at www.cliffsnotes.com. Here's what you find:

■ Interactive tools that are fun and informative

■ Links to interesting Web sites

■ Additional resources to help you continue your learning

At www.cliffsnotes.com, you can even register for a new feature called CliffsNotes Daily, which offers you newsletters on a variety of topics, delivered right to your e-mail inbox each business day.

If you haven't yet discovered the Internet and are wondering how to get online, pick up *Getting on the Internet,* new from CliffsNotes. You'll learn just what you need to make your online connection quickly and easily. See you at www.cliffsnotes.com!

CHAPTER 1

HOW LIFE INSURANCE DIFFERS FROM OTHER TYPES OF INSURANCE

IN THIS CHAPTER

- ■ Dispelling life insurance myths
- ■ Looking at the purposes of life insurance

Life insurance is simple, right? You buy a policy to protect your family, you die, your family gets some money. Simple. Direct. Easy.

Not so fast. Life insurance is much more complicated than that. This chapter describes some of the myths that surround life insurance and takes a look at the main purposes of having a life insurance policy — not just as income for your survivors, but also as part of your investment portfolio, as a tax shelter, and as part of your estate planning.

Myths about Life Insurance

The following sections work to dispel the three main myths about life insurance.

Myth 1: I only need life insurance if I have kids

Most people think that they need life insurance only if they have a family — to ensure that their survivors aren't left hanging if they die prematurely.

Life insurance is important for several other reasons, which you can read about in greater detail later in this chapter. Briefly, these other purposes are income replacement for a spouse to help him or her through a difficult adjustment period, as an investment, as a tax shelter, and as an estate planning tool.

Myth 2: Life insurance is a bad investment

Life insurance may not be the most profitable investment you can make with your money, but rarely is it a bad one. If you measure an investment only in how much you get in return, life insurance may or may not be a good investment. When you buy a life insurance policy, you put money into an account that will pay your survivors that same money, a portion of that money, or that money plus more when you die. If your survivors get more than you put in (or more than what the money could have earned elsewhere), life insurance is a good investment. If your survivors get less, it isn't such a good investment.

However, life insurance is much more than return on investment. Life insurance provides

- Protection for your dependents
- Peace of mind for you

If you're looking for a pure return on capital, you can find many more lucrative investments — even tax-deferred or tax-free options — that can yield considerably more than your life insurance policy. But the primary function of insurance is not as an investment but as protection. No other investment can offer the same amount of protection.

Myth 3: Life insurance is unnecessary for older people

Not very long ago, older meant "over 50." But many people need life insurance at 50, 55, 60, or 65. Age is not always a reason to abandon life insurance. Even so-called "older" people may need income protection for their survivors if these heads of household or primary caregivers die prematurely. People in their 50s and 60s (and sometimes into their 70s) are in their peak earnings years and have family responsibilities.

Remember

You may want to give your loved ones the time to adjust to your death without having to change their normal standards of living. Today, many more people in their 50s and 60s are still supporting young children. If a woman has a child when she's 40 or 42, for example, that child won't finish college until Mom's at least 62. Or suppose you have a non-working spouse and you die at the age of 60; he or she may not be able to find a job that brings in a comparable income to maintain the same standard of living.

Many older people actually need *more* life insurance for a number of reasons:

- You may have less time to make up for the loss of income.

- You may find that inflation has cut into the value of the life insurance benefit.

- You have a greater need for estate planning as you get older because you have less time to carry out your plan.

- You have a greater need for tax planning as you age because you'll most likely earn more, and life insurance can play a significant part in your tax planning.

The Purposes of Life Insurance

The number one reason to have life insurance is, obviously, to protect your beneficiaries if you die prematurely. That's clear. Every other reason is secondary — although for some people, the other purposes can take on greater importance in certain situations.

Providing protection for beneficiaries

Protecting your survivors means replacing the income you bring in if you die prematurely. If you have children, you probably spend your earnings on the costs of bringing them up. If you die, your life insurance death benefit replaces those earnings so that they won't have to suffer financially. If you have a mortgage on your house, a life insurance death benefit can help your family stay in their home if you die.

Remember

Life insurance can help you overcome the difficulty of having to totally change your way of life because you lose half or more of your income.

Lastly, if you are part-owner in a business, the business may purchase a life insurance policy on you so that if you die, your partner can use that death benefit to buy out your share of the business from your heirs.

Using life insurance as an investment

A second purpose of having life insurance is to use it as part of your investment portfolio. Most financial advisors encourage you to balance your investments so that if one kind of investment goes down (the stock market, for example), another one will likely go up (bonds or real estate, perhaps). By balancing your portfolio and diversifying your investments, you can weather storms in one area by having some assets in the other areas that go up or stay level.

Some life insurance policies are actually long-term investments, which you can contribute to and withdraw funds from before you die. These so-called *cash-value policies* — whole life (see Chapter 5) and universal life insurance (see Chapter 6) — are actually savings accounts that accrue a cash value over time and also pay for your protection. Although these policies don't command the highest interest rates you can find, they are untaxed earnings, so you get a higher return than simply putting your money in a savings account on which you must pay taxes.

Using life insurance as a tax shelter

Life insurance can play two roles as a tax-sheltered investment:

■ The earnings on a cash-value policy are not taxed until you take them out.

■ The proceeds of a death benefit settlement are not taxable to your survivors.

Your cash-value account yields tax-deferred income, which, in effect, increases the yield. Take a look at the example illustrated in Figure 1-1.

Figure 1-1:   Comparing two ways to invest $1,000.

$1,000 savings	at	5% interest rate	=	$50 interest yield	−	$14 (28% income tax bracket)	=	$36 yield (3.6%)
$1,000 tax-deferred account (such as a whole life or universal life insurance policy)	at	4% interest rate	=	$40	−	$0 (no taxes)	=	$40 yield (4%)

Now look at the fact that the death benefit is not taxable to your survivors, and using the same logic, compare the taxable versus the non-taxable return: Suppose that you currently earn $60,000 a year, and you buy a $180,000 life insurance policy to help your survivors through three years without your income. If you die, your survivors get the full $180,000, and none of it is taxed.

Although the examples may seem a bit complicated, the point is simple. Because the proceeds of a death settlement and the earnings of a cash-value life insurance policy are both tax-deferred, they serve as excellent tax shelters.

Using life insurance as part of your estate planning

In addition to serving as a tax shelter for you and your survivors, life insurance can also be an important part of *estate planning* — that is, dealing with how to distribute your wealth after you die.

Currently, the federal tax laws state that the first $650,000 in inheritance is federally tax-exempt (that amount increases over the next few years — see Chapter 3). Most states allow the same amount or they have no inheritance tax at all. Realistically, most people don't need to worry much about taxes eating away their estate. Furthermore, most couples own their property and assets jointly, so surviving spouses or owners don't have to pay inheritance taxes, even if the estate is greater than the amount allowed under the law.

But if your estate *is* worth more than the law allows, how do you ensure that your wealth goes to your survivors and not to the government? That's where life insurance and life insurance trusts come in.

To do this sort of estate planning, consult an expert who can both counsel you and set up the appropriate vehicles. Briefly, here's how it works:

1. You set up an *irrevocable life insurance trust,* to which you contribute annually. The trust is, in effect, a life insurance policy, which goes to your children or survivors tax-free. You can't withdraw that money for any reason (hence the term *irrevocable*).

2. You and your spouse each leave to your children whatever the law allows at the time, so that money is also tax-free.

3. You will the remaining amount to a qualified charity of your choice, which, by definition, is exempt from inheritance taxes. If you don't will the remaining amount to a charity, it is considered part of your estate, and your heirs have to pay taxes on it.

In this situation, you take the IRS out of this picture. Using some of your estate, you buy a tax-free life insurance policy so that your heirs get the same amount they would have before any estate taxes — the amount equivalent to your estate. Plus, you donate a large portion of your estate to a charity rather than to the government. The only party that loses is the IRS (and another party wins — the life insurance company, which charges you a significant amount for that policy over a period of years). But your heirs lose nothing! Isn't that the goal of estate planning?

Don't try to wade through this complicated process by yourself. A qualified professional can help you sort through the fine details and prevent you from making a costly mistake.

CHAPTER 2

HOW MUCH LIFE INSURANCE DO YOU NEED?

IN THIS CHAPTER

- Determining your personal economics

- Understanding your survivors' needs

- Dealing with your age

After you understand the purposes of life insurance (see Chapter 1) and decide that you need a life insurance policy, the next step is determining how much protection you should buy. This chapter shows you how to determine how much life insurance you need by explaining how to judge the economic value of your life and your survivors' needs. This chapter also includes a worksheet so that you can make your calculations.

The Economics of Your Life

The basic step in determining how much life insurance you need is to figure out just how much your life is worth. When looking at the economic value of your life, focus on three things:

- Your income

- Your cost of living

- Any uninsured medical costs

Your income

The value of your income is relatively easy to calculate: It's the amount of money you earn, plus the amount of money you'd expect to earn if you hadn't died prematurely. But this figure can be difficult to determine accurately. For one thing, many people have little idea of what they may be earning five years from now, especially younger people who may not have settled into a career yet. Secondly, more and more people change careers (not just jobs, but careers) numerous times in their lives. The average number of careers (again, not jobs) for people is now over five! How can anyone possibly say what his or her income will be in 15 years?

Your best bet when figuring the value of your income is to estimate how much your annual salary is likely to increase each year. When completing the worksheet in this chapter, use an increase of about 5 percent per year. You can see an example of how your salary may grow in Figure 2-1. If you know your salary increases will be more than 5 percent per year, use the higher figure. If you know your increases will be less than 5 percent, use the lower number. You can round off later in the final formula when you determine how much life insurance you need.

Figure 2-1: Estimating salary increases for the future.

				Years from now			
		5	**10**	**15**	**20**	**25**	**30**
	20,000	25,526	32,578	41,579	53,066	67,727	86,439
Current salary	**30,000**	38,288	48,867	62,368	79,599	101,591	129,658
	40,000	51,051	65,156	83,157	106,132	135,454	172,878
	50,000	63,814	81,445	103,946	132,665	169,318	216,097
	60,000	76,577	97,734	124,736	159,198	203,181	259,317
	70,000	89,340	114,023	145,525	185,731	237,045	302,536

Estimated Salary Increases at 5% Annually

Don't forget that in five or ten years, you may quite possibly be working for a different organization or in a different job. If you underestimate your increases, you're also underestimating the amount of income protection that your survivors need.

Your cost of living

The economic value of your life is not only how much you will be earning but also the cost of living — that is, how much you actually *need* to live on. More importantly, the cost of living you and your family have set up is really the amount of life insurance income protection you need to purchase — especially because most people tend to spend a bit more than they bring in.

In addition, part of your living costs are more than likely going into some sort of savings — to pay college expenses when your children are old enough, to go toward your retirement, to cover a big vacation, and so on. You still want your survivors to be able to save for some of these items (college expenses, for example). But clearly, saving for your retirement isn't something you have to be concerned about if you die.

The budget worksheet that follows can help you determine your cost of living. Note that most of your expenses increase over the years due to inflation, if nothing else. On the other hand, some expenses may decrease or be eliminated because they are no longer necessary. One of these, of course, is the life insurance premium. But some other examples of unnecessary costs are clothing, food, and other expenses for children who will eventually be out on their own and paying their own expenses.

Note also that this budget doesn't include unusual expenses, either planned (such as college expenses or weddings, unless your budget includes saving for them) or unexpected (such as medical emergencies or funerals).

And note, finally, that the budget worksheet doesn't include paying off any large debts which you're currently paying over time. If you want your life insurance to pay off some or all of these debts, make sure that you increase the death benefit to cover these amounts so that your survivors no longer have to include the debt payments in their budgets.

Your uninsured medical costs

Uninsured medical costs are one of the biggest potential drains on a family budget. Including uninsured medical costs in your family budget is crucial because health insurance terms, benefits, and regulations change so quickly.

Moreover, because life insurance protection is related to your health, by definition you want to be certain that your survivors can pay for your medical costs should you die. So after completing the budget worksheet, add a flat amount at the bottom to pay for these unexpected and uninsured medical costs.

How much to add? Good question. The figure you decide on will vary depending on what kind of health insurance you have now. If you belong to an HMO, most of your medical expenses are covered. On the other hand, if you have a private plan in which you pay 20 percent of the costs, your portion is likely to be far greater. Only you can really estimate this amount. However, most experts say that you should always maintain approximately three months worth of living expenses available, so try adding that amount to the bottom of the worksheet as your emergency fund to cover these uninsured medical costs.

Budget Worksheet: Expenses

Fixed Expenses

Household:	Rent/Mortgage	_____
	Property Tax/Escrow	_____
	Lawn and tree service	_____
	Domestic help	_____
Insurance:	Homeowners/renters insurance	_____
	Life insurance	_____
	Automobile insurance	_____
	Health/disability insurance	_____
Loans:	Automobile	_____
	Other fixed loans or credit	_____
		_____
		_____

Total Fixed Expenses _____

Variable Expenses

Household:	Utilities (gas, electric, water, sewer)	_____
	Home repair	_____
	Telephone	_____
	Groceries	_____
Transportation:	Auto licenses and registration	_____
	Auto gas and oil	_____
	Auto repair	_____
	Parking	_____
Medical:	Doctors/dentists	_____
	Prescriptions	_____
	Over the counter drugs	_____
Clothing:	Laundry/cleaning	_____
	New purchases	_____

Personal Care:	Toiletries	_____
	Haircuts/styling	_____
	Miscellaneous	_____
Personal:	Dining out	_____
	Entertainment	_____
	Gifts	_____
	Subscriptions and books	_____
	Donations	_____
Miscellaneous:	Bank charges	_____
	Investment expenses	_____
	Legal and professional fees	_____
	Taxes	_____
	Other	_____

Total Variable Expenses   _____

TOTAL EXPENSES (fixed plus variable)   _____

Budget Worksheet: Income

Fixed income

Wages	_____
Dividends	_____
Certificates of deposit	_____
Fixed interest-bearing bank accounts	_____
Rental income	_____
Child support/alimony	_____

Variable income

Capital gains/losses	_____

Continued

Budget Worksheet: Income *(continued)*

Variable income

Variable-interest bank accounts	_____
Tax refunds	_____
Gifts	_____
Other benefits (assign monetary value)	_____
Total Variable Income	_____
TOTAL INCOME (fixed plus variable)	_____

Your Survivors' Needs

The next step in determining how much life insurance you should buy is to decide just how much your survivors need. You need to account for four expenses that your survivors will need to cover:

- Estate taxes
- Probate costs
- The cost of dying
- Planned future expenses

Estate taxes

Depending on the size of your estate, your heirs may have to pay taxes on the amount they inherit. If your entire estate goes to your spouse, he or she faces no tax consequence, regardless of the estate's size.

If, however, your estate goes to other beneficiaries and your estate is larger than the amount allowed under the tax law, your heirs have to pay taxes on the balance over those amounts. Although the 1999 figure of $650,000 may seem huge to you, many people own homes that have increased in value so much that the equity in their home is over the limits allowed by federal inheritance tax law. In these types of situations, heirs may have to pay a significant sum in taxes. Quite likely, they won't have the cash or other liquid assets to pay the estate taxes, particularly if the inheritance is in a form that they can't easily convert to cash. In that case, they either have to sell the asset or pay the estate taxes from other sources.

You can help your heirs pay the inheritance taxes by buying a higher amount of life insurance (and thus a higher death benefit). Be sure to include an amount to cover the estate taxes when you complete the worksheet to determine the amount of protection you need.

Probate

Probate is the process by which your estate is accounted for, all debts and taxes are paid, and whatever is left over goes to the rightful heirs. At this point, your will is officially registered and the executor of your estate is given the legal right to dispose of your assets.

Many executors choose to get assistance from an attorney to handle the financial affairs (although doing so isn't required). Depending on the size of the estate, an attorney may charge $2,000 to $3,000 to handle probate. You may want to increase your life insurance death benefit by that amount to take care of the probate expenses.

Dealing with estates and probate can sometimes get fairly complicated. Speak to an attorney before handling them yourself.

The cost of dying

The cost of dying refers to the expenses of funerals, burials, and the disposal of your body. How much you pay for these expenses is more than likely up to your survivors. The cost of funerals varies enormously. But on average, burials cost between $5,000 and $10,000. Cremations cost considerably less, from $2,000 to $5,000. When determining the amount of life insurance to purchase, consider including an amount in the death benefit that can cover the cost of the funeral.

Talk with your spouse, if you have one, or to your parents if they are your survivors, or your children if they are old enough, about funeral expenses. This conversation may not be easy, but be persistent so that they can honor your wishes (and make theirs known) should you die.

Many funeral homes won't require payment directly from your survivors but will allow and will help you arrange to be paid directly from the life insurance proceeds.

Future expenses

When calculating the needs of your survivors, building in expenses that you know will occur is extremely important. These expenses are usually the largest factors in determining how much insurance to buy.

One of the most obvious of these planned future expenses is the cost of attending college. Build in a cost of about $80,000 to $100,000 per child in today's dollars. Of course, the actual amount your child needs will probably be considerably more later on, which is taken into account with the inflation factor in the worksheet or in the insurance policy.

The amount of life insurance you buy now is the amount your survivors need if you die soon. If you're worried about inflation eating into the death benefit, you can buy an insurance policy in which the death benefit increases in value. You can read more about these kinds of policies in Chapters 5 and 6.

You may be aware of other expenses that your family will incur, such as orthodontia, summer camps, special classes for your children, or special medical needs. You should build these expenses into the worksheets.

Additionally, you can count on at least one or two of those unexpected expenditures that come up, including a new roof for the house, a new car, and medical emergencies for which your health insurance doesn't pay the entire cost. When you complete the budget worksheet, build in some "fudge factor" — about 10 percent of your annual income is good — to account for these unplanned costs.

Age — Yours and Your Survivors'

One of the determinants of how much life insurance to buy is age — your age and the age of your survivors.

Life expectancy

The amount of insurance you purchase depends very much on your life circumstances, what your style of living is, how much your survivors need, and what lies ahead for your beneficiaries.

If you are 30 years old and in good health, the chances are great that you will live another 50 years or more. As medical advancements continue, your life span may be even greater, assuming that you're not hit by that proverbial truck.

Your life span affects your life insurance needs in these ways:

■ The younger you are, the longer your survivors are going to need income replacement, the more dollars you need to put away for future expenses such as your children's education, and the more likely it is that your living expenses are lower.

■ The older you are, the less chance your spouse has to plan for his or her retirement, the less likely it is that your survivors will have to depend on you to fund a college education, and the more likely your spouse is to need medical, skilled-care assistance, or nursing home care.

Cost of premiums

The age at which you buy life insurance relates directly to the cost of your *premium* (the amount you must pay for the coverage). The younger you are, the cheaper the premium. A 38-year-old male buying a five-year, term life insurance policy with a death benefit of $100,000 may pay only about $175 per year, while a 48-year-old may have to pay about twice that amount for the same coverage.

If, however, that 38-year-male old wants to buy a cash-value life insurance policy — one that not only provides a death benefit when he dies but also builds some value that he can use when he retires (or that adds to the death benefit) — he may have to pay about $600 a year, about three-quarters of which goes into his cash-value account.

When determining how much life insurance you need, you have to take into account how much life insurance you can *afford*. The cost of insurance goes up every year as you age because your life expectancy is lower and the insurance company knows it has fewer years before you are expected to die. Decide how much you can afford to pay per year and work with that amount to determine how much life insurance to buy.

One way to estimate how much your premiums will be in five or ten years is to find out what the premium would be now if you were five or ten years older. Doing so gives you the price in today's dollars. You can add about 15 to 20 percent more for five years and about 40 to 50 percent more for ten years to account for inflation.

CHAPTER 3

LIFE INSURANCE IN ESTATE PLANNING

IN THIS CHAPTER

- Naming beneficiaries
- Setting up trusts
- Tracking your dividends, rates of return, and annuities
- Looking into viatical settlements

Although income protection for their survivors is clearly the main reason that most people buy life insurance, estate planning is a close second. The goal of estate planning is to ensure not only the smooth distribution of your wealth to your heirs, but also that the government doesn't take too big a bite. And the wealthier you are, the bigger the tax bite. This chapter looks at the role that life insurance plays in planning for your retirement, including dividends, annuities, and tax consequences. The chapter also focuses on how life insurance can help ensure a seamless transfer of your estate to your heirs.

Beneficiaries

When you purchase a life insurance policy, one of the first things you must do is decide who will be the recipient of the benefits — hence the term *beneficiaries.* Most people designate their spouse as the primary beneficiary, which means that the spouse gets the entire death benefit when the policyholder dies. If you're single, your primary beneficiary is likely to be your children, if you have any.

However, your circumstances may give you reason to name more than one beneficiary, especially if your estate is sizable.

Naming additional beneficiaries is extremely important in the event that the primary beneficiary dies at the same time you do or that person dies before you.

The following sections outline four reasons why you may (or may not) choose to name someone other than your spouse or children as your beneficiary.

Minor children

You may not want to choose your children as your beneficiaries if they are still minors.

Under the current law, children under the age of 18 can't collect insurance benefits directly, even if they're the rightful heirs. If you die and your children are the beneficiaries, the proceeds can only go to them in a trust fund, which an adult must manage. If you don't select this adult (perhaps a lawyer or an accountant, or an organization such as a bank), the probate court selects someone or some organization to oversee the money. When your children reach the age of maturity, usually 18 years old, the funds automatically go to them. Before that time, the trust fund administrator controls how the funds are invested and spent.

Avoiding tax consequences

As Chapter 1 points out, estates larger than $650,000 (in 1999) may face some potential tax consequences. (This *applicable exclusion amount,* as it's called, is set to increase over the next several years, as illustrated in Figure 3-1.) The first $650,000 can go to your beneficiaries tax-free, but your heirs (excluding your spouse) have to pay income taxes on anything over that amount. If you have a large estate, you may want to ensure that more of your estate goes into your beneficiary's hands, rather than to the government.

Figure 3-1: The tax-free portion of your estate will increase to $1 million in 2006.

Year	Applicable Exclusion Amount
1998	$625,000
1999	$650,000
2000	$675,000
2001	$675,000
2002	$700,000
2003	$700,000
2004	$850,000
2005	$950,000
2006 & thereafter	$1,000,000

Spreading the wealth

You may also stray from the norm when selecting your beneficiaries if you want to donate part of your estate to charity.

For business owners

Owning a business may be another reason you choose beneficiaries other than family members. Some business owners who are in partnerships arrange to have the proceeds of their life insurance policy tied to the price of the business. When an owner dies and the death benefit goes to the family (the heirs), that death benefit becomes the payment for the deceased's share of the business. In this way, the other partners can buy the business without having to negotiate the price.

Trusts

A trust is an account that you set up for someone else but for which you decide the terms. You can set up a trust from your assets or from your life insurance policy, and you can continue to add to it or not. The following sections describe the three kinds of trusts that most affect life insurance policies.

Revocable trusts

A *revocable trust* is a means by which you can allocate your property, including your life insurance death benefit, to another person. You can change the provisions of this trust fund any time during your life, making the trust "revocable." You still manage and have total control of the fund, and you can even abolish it if you choose.

Your minor children can't be the direct beneficiaries of your life insurance death benefit. You must set up a trust fund in their names.

Trusts serve to ensure that certain funds go directly to a beneficiary (your minor children, for example). But you can also use a trust to save on taxes. For example, you can set up a *bypass trust,* which allows you to pass some of your estate on to your grandchildren, thereby "bypassing" any tax consequence to your children.

Because of the legal and tax implications, consult an attorney if you are considering setting up any sort of trust.

Irrevocable trusts

An *irrevocable trust,* as its name implies, means that you cannot amend, change, or alter the terms of the trust. The trust becomes a legal entity unto itself and, in that sense, has certain rights. People commonly use irrevocable trusts to make large gifts to children, grandchildren, and even great-grandchildren without creating any liability for estate taxes.

The tax law permits giving any one individual (or any one irrevocable trust) $10,000 per person per year without that individual having to pay taxes on the gift. When you die, the death benefit from an irrevocable trust goes directly to the trust, also with no tax liability.

Remember

Because your spouse pays no estate tax on funds that go to him or her, you need to set up an irrevocable trust only for your children and/or grandchildren.

Charitable remainder trust

As its name implies, a charitable remainder trust fund is set up by people who want to give their property to a charity. The property can come in any form: cash, real estate, stocks, bonds, or the proceeds from a life insurance policy.

The charitable remainder trust has two benefits:

■ The charity or organization you choose gets the property.

■ Your heirs aren't responsible for any taxes on the appreciated value of the property, if the property value has increased (and it probably has). Of course, this benefit is only important if your estate is valued at over the $650,000 exemption.

Rates of Return

The two basic forms of life insurance policies (which I cover in greater detail in the following chapters) are *term life* — in which you buy protection for a specified period of time (the *term*) — and cash-value. With cash-value insurance policies, you pay more than just the cost of the premium into an account that is yours and accrues interest. In effect, cash-value policies are like a savings plan.

For a life insurance policy to be part of your estate planning, you must know your *rate of return* — how much interest your money earns.

When a company quotes you a price for a cash-value policy, it also quotes a guaranteed rate of return. At the same time, you will likely be given one or two other rates of return and will be shown charts and tables demonstrating how much your money will yield after just a few years.

Be very wary of these tactics. Don't think you'll make a killing! Assume your money will earn very close to the guaranteed minimum, and consider anything over the guaranteed minimum as a bonus.

The return you receive from your cash-value policy is to

■ Increase your *surrender value* (the amount that you can expect to receive if you withdraw the funds)

■ Increase your death benefit

■ Pay the expected increase in the cost of your protection each year

Dividends

Many insurance companies are *mutual companies,* meaning that the policyholders own the company's stock. When the insurance company does well, the owners receive dividends. The amount of the dividend relates directly to how well the company performs.

Dividends from mutual insurance companies go directly to lowering the premiums. These dividends can be quite substantial, as high as 50 to 70 percent of the premium.

You can't count on getting this dividend each year. However, with term insurance, you buy only one term at a time. So if the insurance company doesn't declare a dividend consistently, you can look elsewhere for a better rate from a company that does offer a dividend. On the other hand, you don't want to constantly jump from one company to the next. For one thing, you can't always be sure that you'll qualify for the life insurance. So choosing the right company at the very beginning is one of the most important decisions you will make. Read Chapter 8 and select a good life insurance company that you know will be around for a while.

Annuities

Most people think of life insurance as the primary way of protecting survivors or heirs. However, some life insurance policies, called *annuities,* provide an income to the insured person later on in life. Annuities are basically investment vehicles in which you plop down a bunch of money, either as a lump sum or in years of payments, in exchange for a promise from an insurance company that it will pay you a monthly income, usually after a defined period. Of course, that period won't arrive until well after the company has received enough money from you to make paying you financially viable for them. Two types of annuities are available:

- **Fixed annuities:** With a *fixed annuity,* the company pays you a guaranteed rate of growth, based on the amount you have paid in premiums and the terms you have agreed upon beforehand. These payments can be either for a set number of years or until you die.

- **Variable annuities:** With *variable annuities,* you can direct how and where the money is invested. The amount you're paid varies depending on how successful you and the company's investment funds are. You can instruct the company to invest in any combination of funds that the company offers — stock funds, bond funds, fixed income funds, or other investment funds. Most insurance companies that offer annuities offer a pretty wide array of funds from which to choose, ranging from growth stock funds to global investment funds. Some are higher risk, some lower.

As an investment opportunity, annuities aren't the greatest options. You can usually do better in other funds and with other accounts. However, with an annuity, you're investing and being insured at the same time, which may be an attractive benefit for you.

Viatical Settlements

Life insurance offers a relatively new benefit called *viatical settlements,* which may affect your estate planning. With this program, terminally ill patients can, in effect, "sell" the proceeds of their life insurance death benefit to a third party and receive the cash they need while they're alive.

To qualify for this benefit, your doctor must certify that your life expectancy is no more than two years based on the fact that you have a terminal disease. The company then purchases your life insurance policy (including any cash value) for 60 percent of the face value. If your disease has progressed even further, and your doctors certify that you have less than six months, the viatical company will purchase your life insurance policy for up to 80 percent of the face value.

The purpose of the settlement is to ensure that terminally ill patients have the bulk of their life insurance benefit available to pay for their medical and living costs. On the other hand, terminally ill people must decide whether the life insurance benefits are for them or for their survivors.

As you would expect, this issue is fairly controversial. You can learn more about this kind of policy by checking with an insurance company that offers viatical settlements. You should also check out the information made available by the Federal Trade Commission (FTC), which you can reach by writing Federal Trade Commission, P.O. Box P, Room 403, Washington, DC 20580, or its Web site at www.ftc.gov/bcp/online/viatical.htm.

CHAPTER 4
TERM INSURANCE

Some say that every type of life insurance is term insurance: For all forms of life insurance, you pay each year. The only difference between term insurance and all the others is whether you pay the premiums directly (as with term life insurance) or the payment comes out of the earnings from an investment that the insurance company holds (as with other types of life insurance). In this chapter I discuss the attributes of term life insurance that distinguish it from the other forms. I cover the various provisions that differentiate each attribute and each type of term life insurance.

Understanding Term Insurance

Term insurance is the most basic form of life insurance and, therefore, the easiest to understand. At its simplest level, term insurance provides life insurance for a defined period (usually a one-, five-, or ten-year term). For that insurance, you pay a monthly, quarterly, annual, or semiannual premium that remains constant during the specified term.

But that's pretty much the only constant. I can't even say that the death benefit remains the same for the entire term of the policy because various options are available, such as *decreasing term insurance* and *increasing term insurance,* in which the death benefit changes each year (rarely more than 20 percent above or below the original policy amount). These two products are distinguished from *level term insurance,* in which the death benefit remains the same for a specified period.

Term insurance provides a benefit for others if you die during the specified period. Term insurance is *not* an investment — you receive no benefits other than the security of knowing that if you die, the insurance proceeds go to your beneficiaries.

Exploring Options in Term Insurance

Although term insurance is no more than a policy for a defined period, it comes in many different forms, and you have various options when choosing a policy. The options you must consider are discussed in the following sections.

Renewable term

The primary purpose of life insurance is so that your beneficiaries receive a benefit if you die. If you buy life insurance, not only do you want your policy to remain in effect during the specific period you designated, but you also want to be able to keep buying the insurance until *you* decide to stop — not when the company decides that you've become too great a risk.

Most term life policies are renewable — but your premium may not be the same for the renewed period. (I discuss premiums in Chapter 9.) After each term (the one-, five-, or ten-year period that you specified) ends, the amount you pay per year for the next term will increase.

A policy may be renewable only for a limited time (ten years, for example). So when shopping for a policy, be sure to check for how long it is renewable.

Without renewability, the insurance company can decide that it no longer wants to insure you when the term of your policy ends. Renewable term insurance insures that you can still buy life insurance regardless of the condition of your health later; after you qualify the first time, you don't have to take any additional medical exams to maintain your policy. And because you become a bigger health risk as you age, not passing a medical exam is the danger of not purchasing a renewable policy.

Renewable doesn't mean that you can change the face amount of your policy. If you decide that you want more insurance, the company will likely require that you pass a new medical exam to qualify.

Age limits

Many term insurance policies have an age limit (specified in your contract) after which the company won't allow you to renew your policy. This age can range from as low as 60 years old to 85, 90, or even older. Obviously, at the upper age ranges most people are extremely high risks, so the price of coverage would be so high that it wouldn't pay for you to purchase coverage. But certainly 60 or 70 isn't very old, and many people at that age want continued coverage.

When looking at term insurance policies, make sure you give consideration to any age limits imposed in the policy.

Convertible term

If you purchase a *convertible* policy, you are allowed to convert to a different type of policy — one that builds a cash value, such as whole life or universal life, which I discuss in

Chapters 5 and 6 — without having to pass another medical exam. Again, because your health is more likely to deteriorate as you age, this feature may be important if you think that you may want to keep buying life insurance later in life.

Most people don't continue to insure themselves after they reach retirement age, usually because they no longer have anyone dependent upon them, but there are exceptions. For example, take a look at a family of four in which the father is 56, the mother is 43, and the two children are both under 10. The younger child won't start college for another 15 years, and the parents want to make sure the children have sufficient money even if the father dies. These parents may want to keep insuring the father after he reaches the age of 70, the age at which his policy specifies that he can no longer renew his term insurance policy. To them, therefore, convertibility is an important option.

Another reason you may want to be able to convert your term insurance is if your family has a history of heart disease, cancer, or other serious illness. If your family history makes you more likely to become sick later in life, you may want to ensure that you don't have to pass a medical exam later, even after term insurance is not available. Because buying life insurance is, basically, eliminating as much risk as possible, many people think that this provision is an important one.

A third reason to keep the convertible option has to do with the price of term policies versus cash-value policies. Term policies generally cost considerably less than other types of life insurance because the others also build value while paying for the insurance. Convertibility may be important to you if you're on a limited budget but want a cash-value policy. You know that you can convert later, when you have greater financial strength.

Remember

Keeping the option to convert means that your policy will likely cost you more.

Consider the following questions regarding convertibility:

■ **To what can you convert your policy?** Whole life? Universal life? Either one? Any product the company offers later on?

■ **When can you convert?** Some policies specify how many years you have to convert. Obviously, more time to decide gives you more options when you need them. Of course, the additional flexibility likely means a higher premium throughout the life of the term policy.

■ **When you do decide to convert, will the new premium be based on your age when you convert?** Or will the company require you to make a lump sum payment to "catch up," as though you had purchased the cash value policy to begin with?

Decreasing term

For most term insurance policies, the death benefit remains constant and the premium increases over time. With a decreasing term life policy, the opposite is true: After the specified term, the face value of the policy decreases, while the amount you pay each year or month remains the same. In that way, the insurance company effectively increases its premium, which it must do because, as you age, you're at a greater risk for death. So the same premium purchases an increasingly lower amount of insurance.

For many people, decreasing term life insurance allows them to be insured to the maximum when they most need it (when their beneficiaries are most dependent on them) but to be insured for lower amounts as their beneficiaries need less. Because the premiums remain locked in, budgeting is simple — you always pay the same amount.

Mortgage insurance is an example of decreasing term insurance. When you buy mortgage insurance, you're making sure that your home mortgage gets paid off if you die. But of course, while you're alive, you're paying off your mortgage principal, so the balance keeps declining.

Re-entry term

Renewable term insurance may have a provision called *re-entry*, which means that the insurance company can ask you to undergo a medical exam before it will renew your policy after the term expires. If your health isn't good and the re-entry clause permits it, the company can cancel your insurance. In return, you can purchase renewed insurance at a reduced rate — basically, the rate a person who just passed an exam would pay.

The gamble here is that you will remain healthy. Then again, if the re-entry clause doesn't permit the company to cancel your insurance but does allow it to charge you higher premiums, you're gambling on money, not your health. Some re-entry policies spell out the maximum premium that can be charged. If you're gambling, you ought to know how much you're gambling on.

When purchasing re-entry term insurance, make sure that you keep the right to renew your insurance even if you don't pass a medical exam. Although may have to pay higher premiums, at least the company won't be able to cancel your policy.

Employee benefits

Many companies offer term life insurance policies to their employees as a fringe benefit. The amount often ranges from the equivalent of your annual salary to triple your annual salary. The employer usually pays the entire premium.

Warning

Only the cost of the first $50,000 in life insurance is tax-free. Any premium an employer pays on your behalf for an insurance policy over $50,000 is additional income that you must claim on your tax return. In addition, this benefit is available to you only while you are employed with the company. When you leave, you lose the protection. If having that insurance was part of your estate planning, you now have to reevaluate your position.

Summing Up

To help you put term life insurance in perspective and determine whether it's a product that you should consider, Table 4-1 lists the pros and cons of this type of insurance.

Table 4-1: Pros and Cons of Term Insurance

Pros	*Cons*
At a young age, term insurance is considerably less expensive than cash-value policies are.	Term insurance becomes more expensive as you age. In addition, the dividends you receive are often much less than what the company pays to cash-value policyholders.
All the money you pay goes toward the death benefit policy. None goes to cash value.	If you outlive the term, the policy has no cash value.
Very little of what you pay goes toward commissions.	Insurance agents don't often encourage people to buy term policies because they make more money off cash-value policies.
Term insurance is simple to understand and does exactly what it is meant to do: protect your beneficiaries.	No tax advantages. In addition, due to inflation, a death benefit that remains constant actually declines in purchasing value because the dollars buy less later on. So in effect, the protection is less.

Comparing Term Insurance Policies

If you decide that term insurance is for you, the next step is to get quotes from at least three insurance companies and compare them. To help you, I've provided a worksheet for you to fill out. Step 2 of the worksheet asks you to find out the rating of the insurance company — see Chapter 8 for more information about ratings companies, and see the Resource Center in this book for how to obtain ratings.

Term Insurance Worksheet

		Company 1	Company 2	Company 3
1.	Name of company	_____	_____	_____
2.	Rating of insurance company			
	Rating from company 1	_____	_____	_____
	Rating from company 2	_____	_____	_____
	Rating from company 3	_____	_____	_____
3.	Initial death benefit/ amount of insurance (Use the same amount for each company for easy comparison)	_____	_____	_____
4.	1st year premium	_____	_____	_____
5.	Guaranteed 1st year dividend	_____	_____	_____
6.	Total paid first year (line 4 minus line 5)	_____	_____	_____
7.	5th year premium	_____	_____	_____
8.	Estimated 5th year dividend	_____	_____	_____
9.	Total paid 5th year (line 7 minus line 8)	_____	_____	_____
10.	10th year premium	_____	_____	_____

Continued

Term Insurance Worksheet *(continued)*

		Company 1	Company 2	Company 3
11.	Estimated 10th year dividend	_____	_____	_____
12.	Total paid 10th year (line 10 minus line 11)	_____	_____	_____
13.	Additional cost for options			
	Renewability	_____	_____	_____
	Convertibility	_____	_____	_____
	Re-entry	_____	_____	_____
	Other	_____	_____	_____
14.	Other options			
	Age limit?	_____	_____	_____
	Decreasing term?	_____	_____	_____
15.	Additional cost if placed in a higher-risk category	_____	_____	_____

CHAPTER 5

WHOLE LIFE INSURANCE

IN THIS CHAPTER

- Understanding cash value
- Looking at traditional whole life
- Exploring interest-sensitive whole life
- Investigating single-premium whole life
- Determining the pros and cons of whole life insurance
- Choosing a whole life insurance policy

Whole life insurance covers you for your entire life, not just a specific period. Your death benefit remains the same, and so does your premium. (With term insurance, your premium increases as you age to account for the fact that you're a bigger health risk.) Insurance companies keep both the premium and the death benefit constant during the life of a whole life policy by charging you a premium that's higher than the cost of the insurance when you're young and using some of that profit to pay for the higher cost of your insurance when you're older.

You can distinguish whole life insurance from term insurance in two significant ways:

- You don't buy insurance for just one year at a time with whole life insurance.
- You build up a cash value with whole life insurance.

Compared to term insurance, therefore, you do seem to get more than you pay for with whole life. But that's not entirely true. In this chapter, I explain how cash value works and illustrate how the concept ties into whole life insurance policies. I also discuss the different kinds of whole life policies, the options you have when purchasing a whole life policy, and the pluses and minuses of whole life versus term insurance. (See Chapter 4 for more information about term insurance.)

Cash Value

Building a cash value means that your life insurance policy has a value greater than just the *death benefit* — the face value of the insurance policy — that goes to your beneficiaries when you die. (With term insurance, the value is *only* the amount of death benefit you sign up for.)

So what's the catch? Why would anyone want term insurance instead of a policy with a value beyond the death benefit? To answer that question, you first need to examine how cash-value whole life insurance works.

The investment concept

When you purchase a whole life policy, a portion of your premium goes toward the life insurance itself, another portion goes toward your cash value, and the rest goes toward administrative costs and your agent's commission.

The insurance company invests the cash-value portion, and in return, you get some of the profits. Your share goes into your cash value. In a sense, then, this portion is an investment. Like all investments, it has its rewards.

Tax benefits

One of the biggest differences between this investment and many others is that *all* of the return on your investment is tax-deferred. You don't have to pay any taxes on this gain until you withdraw it, unlike other investments for which you must pay a capital gains tax. An investment in whole life insurance becomes even more attractive when you consider the following:

- The portion of your premiums that goes toward purchasing your actual insurance reduces the amount of gain you realize.

- You pay taxes only on the difference between the total gain and the total premiums paid, making the return on your investment significantly higher than if you had to pay taxes on the entire thing. (Even the capital gains tax is 20 percent, so if nothing else, you're getting 20 percent more than if you put this same money in an interest-bearing savings account.)

For example, if you get a 5 percent return on a savings account of $10,000, at the end of the year you have $500. But you also have to pay 20 percent of that return in income taxes. In effect, you only gain $400 (20 percent of $500 is $100, which, subtracted from $500, equals $400). In contrast, if the $10,000 is in a tax-deferred account, such as a whole life insurance policy, with an interest of 5 percent, you gain all of the $500. You can see this comparison illustrated in Figure 5-1.

Figure 5-1: Comparing two ways of investing $10,000.

| $10,000 savings | at | 5% interest rate | = | $500 interest yield | − | $100 (20% capital gains tax) | = | $400 yield (4%) |

$$\begin{array}{cccccccc}
\$10,000 & \text{at} & 5\% & = & \$500 & - & \$100 & = & \$400 \\
\text{savings} & & \text{interest rate} & & \text{interest yield} & & (20\% \text{ capital} & & \text{yield} \\
& & & & & & \text{gains tax}) & & (4\%) \\
\end{array}$$

$$\begin{array}{cccccccc}
\$1,000 & \text{at} & 5\% & = & \$500 & - & \$0 & = & \$500 \\
\text{tax-deferred} & & \text{interest rate} & & \text{interest yield} & & (\text{no taxes}) & & \text{yield} \\
\text{account} & & & & & & & & (5\%) \\
(\text{such as a whole} & & & & & & & & \\
\text{life insurance policy}) & & & & & & & & \\
\end{array}$$

If you're considering whole life insurance as a good way to invest, keep in mind that the rate of return you receive historically has been pitifully low, even adding the tax savings back in. Use the protection you're buying, not the rate of return you get, as your basis for judging any type of life insurance as an investment.

Rates of return

The rate of return you get from an investment in whole life insurance is based on the insurance company's ability to invest wisely. The company combines all the cash-value money it gets from all its policyholders and invests this sum, usually in low-risk investments, which naturally pay lower profits than many other investments. Regardless of what return the company gets on its investment, though, most whole life policies guarantee at least a minimum rate of return. Anything the company makes over that (and over and above its costs) goes toward your cash value.

Table 5-1 gives you an example.

Table 5-1: Sample Whole Life Insurance Summary

End of Year	Age	Premium	Total Accrued Premiums	Cash Value (10.75% Example)	Death Benefit	Cash Value (8% Projection)	Cash Value (4% Guarantee)	Cash Value (Actual)*
1	38	$1,596	$1,596	$1,164	$50,000	$1,143	$1,052	$1,084
2	39	612	2,208	1,791	50,000	1,735	1,529	1,529
3	40	612	2,820	2,475	50,000	2,365	2,015	2,016
4	41	612	3,432	3,229	50,000	3,040	2,505	2,560
5	42	612	4,044	4,053	50,000	3,760	3,005	3,137
10	47	612	7,104	9,604	50,000	8,208	5,556	6,466
15	52	612	10,164	18,719	50,000	14,567	8,058	n/a**
20	57	612	13,224	33,861	50,000	23,671	10,207	n/a**
25	62	612	16,284	59,076	50,000	37,005	11,440	n/a**

*The figures in the cash value actual return column are taken from my personal life insurance policy.

**n/a: data not available.

In this example, the insured — a 38-year-old married man — insures himself for $50,000, for which he pays $51 per month ($612 per year). He also begins the policy with an initial investment of $1,596. The company guarantees him a rate of return of 4 percent but shows projections of double and almost triple the return (8 percent and 10.75 percent respectively).

The projections that insurance agents give you are often little more than high hopes, and you shouldn't count on getting anything more than what is guaranteed.

If you look at the actual return, you can see that it's just a bit higher than the minimum guaranty. But it's also significantly lower than either of the more optimistic projections the agent presented. Note that the cash value never exceeds the amount of the premiums paid with the 4 percent guaranteed return (which is just over the minimum). On the other hand — in part because of the initial investment — somewhere around the 10th year, all of the premium paid goes toward the cash value, meaning that the interest on the reserve amount actually covers the cost of the insurance itself.

As you age, the cash value increases at a slower rate because your insurance costs more. From the 20th to the 25th year, for example, this policyholder pays over $4,000 in premiums, but his cash value increases only $1,200. That lower yield reflects the very high cost of purchasing insurance at age 60, indicating that unless you still want a death benefit at that age, you may want to cash out the policy.

Dividends

Over and above the guaranteed rate of return, some companies offer policyholders the opportunity to benefit from the company's success, just like shareholders do. The company pays policyholders dividends, based on how well the company did the previous year. Policies with this benefit are called *participating policies* (often referred to as *par policies* as opposed to *non-par policies* — that is, ones that don't pay dividends).

The amount of your dividend depends on a number of factors:

- The company's overall financial success

- How well the company anticipated interest rates

- The number of claims the company had to pay

- How well the company did in its investments

- The specific terms of your policy

Dividends are factored into complex formulas — the outcome of which is your premium amount — and on the other options the company offers (such as loan benefits), as well as the guaranteed rate of return.

Tip

Some companies pay a *terminal dividend* — a kind of bonus, if you will — upon the policyholder's death. Naturally, a company makes no guaranty that it will pay this dividend (or any dividend, for that matter), and you should consider that possibility when evaluating competing policies. However, most annual and terminal dividends are, indeed, paid.

When the insurance company declares that it will pay a dividend, it can pay the policyholder in cash, use the dividend to pay the cost of the purchased life insurance, put the money into the cash value, or apply the amount toward additional life insurance coverage. The option is usually up to the policyholder, and there are reasons for choosing each option. Naturally, the company hopes you choose to apply the amount toward additional coverage — in fact, most of the illustrations and examples that agents use in their sales presentations select that option.

The portion of an annual dividend paid to you in cash that exceeds the premiums you paid for the year is taxable. A dividend credited to your cash value or applied toward your premium is not taxable until you withdraw funds from the account.

Traditional Whole Life

The following sections look at some of the specific features of traditional whole life insurance.

Death benefit

With whole life, just as with term insurance, your beneficiaries receive only the *death benefit* — the face value of the policy, meaning the protection you purchased — when you die, even though the premiums you paid also contributed toward a cash value. With whole life, none of the cash value you accrue adds to the death benefit because the cash value goes toward paying the higher cost of the insurance as you age.

Termination

If you terminate your whole life insurance, you're entitled to receive a *surrender value,* which is basically the amount of your accrued cash value. The surrender value continues to increase as you continue to contribute to the policy, but as you saw in Table 5-1, the amount increases at a progressively slower rate.

Policy loans

An additional benefit of whole life policies is the fact that you can borrow against your cash value, usually at interest rates significantly lower than market rates — between 6 and 8 percent.

The rates are so low because the lender is assuming absolutely no risk — if you don't pay back the loan, it can take the money from your account. When you borrow against your policy, you don't have to pay any fees, and you can usually get the money in just a few days. If you die before you pay back the loan, the outstanding amount is deducted from the death benefit. If you terminate the policy, the outstanding loan balance is deducted from the cash surrender value.

Interest-Sensitive Whole Life

Interest-sensitive whole life insurance is a whole life policy in which you are paid an adjustable, variable interest, rather than a guaranteed rate. Like an adjustable rate mortgage, the rate you are paid is often tied into an economic indicator such as the Treasury Bill rate.

Premiums, death benefits, and cash value are all aligned with the variable interest rate so that policyholders have various options. When interest rates rise, you can maintain the same death benefit and percentage that goes toward your cash value but lower your premiums. Or you can hold the premium and death benefit steady while increasing your cash value. In some policies you can increase your death benefit while keeping the premium and cash value rate of return steady.

Naturally, the opposite options are also available when interest rates are on the decline: cash-value return decreases while premiums and death benefit are constant; premiums rise so that cash-value return and death benefit remain the same; or death benefit decreases while cash-value return and premiums stay at the same levels.

Interest-sensitive whole life policies are very similar to universal life policies (see Chapter 6).

Single-Premium Whole Life

Some insurance companies offer *single-premium whole life* for people who have a large sum of money available to spend on insurance and who are looking for some tax benefits. You purchase the policy by plunking down one large sum for a specified death benefit. You don't pay any annual premiums, and the death benefit either remains constant or increases, depending on the kind of policy you purchase. The insurance company takes your money up front, invests it, and pays you a small return, similar to what you get with other whole life policies.

Like other whole life policies, a cash value does accrue, usually with a guaranteed minimum return. When the insured dies, the death benefit *plus* any accrued cash value goes to the beneficiaries.

If you're sitting on some cash and you want to buy life insurance, consider this option. In essence, you pay all your premiums up front with single-premium whole life and then let the company have use of your money for the entire period. In exchange, you get a few benefits that may be important to you:

- **You get a substantial discount on the cost of the insurance itself.** Your lump-sum payment is less than the accumulated cost of annual premiums on comparable whole life policies.

- **You get a significant tax savings.** The tax savings may be the primary reason that people purchase this kind of life insurance. All the money you earn on your single-premium whole life policy is tax-deferred.

- **You can immediately borrow against the cash value in your account.** And if you only borrow against what the cash value itself earns, then you will likely pay approximately the same interest the cash value earns, as well. Thus, by storing some money in the company's coffers, you give yourself the opportunity to take out a loan virtually interest-free.

Don't purchase any kind of insurance policy based on the rate of return or tax benefit you receive. If you don't need or want life insurance, you need to look into other, more profitable methods of saving money or lowering your tax burden.

If you borrow against your whole life insurance policy, you need to pay particular attention to the potential tax consequences. If the amount you borrow includes any of the *tax-deferred gain* (the interest you've accrued), you may have to pay taxes on the gain. Check with your tax advisor before exercising this option.

Summing Up

Compare the pros and cons of whole life insurance in Table 5-2.

Table 5-2: Pros and Cons of Whole Life Insurance

Pros	Cons
An increasing amount of the money you pay goes toward your cash value.	Your earnings will most likely be fairly low, probably just a bit more than the amount guaranteed.
The premium remains constant for the entire time you're covered (unless you choose a variable-premium policy).	Higher premium than term insurance because you're also contributing toward your cash value and the agent's higher commission, and because the early premiums subsidize the higher cost of insurance when you're older.

Continued

Table 5-2: Pros and Cons of Whole Life Insurance *(continued)*

Pros	Cons
Your life insurance coverage is totally paid after only a few years by the profits from the cash value.	Not appropriate to use as an investment due to poor rate of return.
Lifelong coverage and no medical exam (unless you make changes to policy).	Death benefit coverage becomes unnecessary later in life when you have no the dependent beneficiaries.
Tax-deferred cash-value earnings, and when you cash out, the premiums you paid reduce the gain.	Returns aren't as high as other tax-deferred plans such as IRAs and 401(k)s, (which also allow you to invest your money wherever you want).

Comparing Whole Life Insurance Policies

If you've decided that whole life insurance is for you, the next step is to get quotes from at least three insurance companies and compare them. To help you, I've provided a worksheet for you to fill out. Step 2 of the worksheet asks you to find out the rating of the insurance company — see Chapter 8 for more information about ratings companies, and see the Resource Center at the back of this book for how to obtain ratings.

Whole Life Insurance Worksheet

		Company 1	Company 2	Company 3
1.	Name of company	_____	_____	_____
2.	Rating of insurance company			
	Rating from company 1	_____	_____	_____
	Rating from company 2	_____	_____	_____

		Company 1	Company 2	Company 3
	Rating from company 3	_____	_____	_____
3.	Initial death benefit/ amount of insurance (Use the same amount for each company for easy comparison)	_____	_____	_____
4.	Annual premium	_____	_____	_____
5.	Guaranteed rate of return	_____	_____	_____
6.	Interest-sensitive policy	_____	_____	_____
	How often can interest rate change?	_____	_____	_____
	Can premium or expenses change?	_____	_____	_____
	Current interest rate	_____	_____	_____
	Previous year's interest rate	_____	_____	_____
7.	Projected surrender value after:			
	1st year	_____	_____	_____
	5th year	_____	_____	_____
	10th year	_____	_____	_____
8.	Dividends			
	Is there a history of dividends?	_____	_____	_____
	Annual estimated dividend	_____	_____	_____
	Terminal estimated dividend	_____	_____	_____
9.	Additional costs if placed in a higher-risk category	_____	_____	_____

CHAPTER 6

UNIVERSAL LIFE INSURANCE

IN THIS CHAPTER

- Understanding universal life

- Learning about interest

- Borrowing against your cash value

- Deciding on death benefits

- Determining premiums

- Determining the pros and cons of universal life insurance

- Choosing a universal life insurance policy

Universal life insurance provides flexibility to policyholders. It's similar to whole life, in that you have a cash value that grows, and it encompasses a term life policy, where you decide the terms and renew the policy annually. However, universal life isn't simple like term insurance — or even like whole life. In fact, balancing the options can be quite complicated. So in this chapter, I discuss the basics of universal life insurance, the elements that you get to compare for your particular needs, and your options in designing the right policy for you.

How Universal Life Works

Universal life insurance is a form of whole life insurance — but with much greater flexibility. Like whole life, you have two components: a term insurance policy and an investment account from which the term insurance premiums are paid. But with universal life, you get to choose your options, and the choices are generally laid out in front of you. You know how the premiums may change the death benefit and cash value, and it's much clearer how much of the premiums go toward your insurance protection, how much toward your cash value, and how much toward administrative expense (including commissions).

Start with a planned death benefit that you work out with your agent. You determine your planned premium, based on how much you can afford and the cost of the insurance. The company subtracts an expense charge based on its fees, usually a fixed percentage of the premiums. You're left with a cash value that generates interest.

But understanding universal life insurance doesn't end there. From the cash value, the company subtracts the current cost of insurance (the *mortality charge*), including the charges for any options (or *riders*), and monthly administrative expenses. Then the company adds in interest that your investment money earns. Your *ending cash value* is the accumulated value that belongs to you when you cash out (or to your beneficiary when you die).

Often, companies charge you a *surrender charge* to cash out, leaving you with the *surrender value.* The surrender charge is usually a small percentage of the total cash value.

Other aspects of universal life to consider include:

■ All the earnings in your investment account are tax-deferred.

■ If you stop paying premiums, the company continues to pay the premium for you by deducting from your policy's cash value. The company does so until no cash value is left. This is one way to continue coverage without paying premiums.

■ The interest rate is a fixed rate, although it may be a *tiered interest rate,* in which part is paid at one rate while the balance is paid at a higher rate. For example, your interest rate may be 4 percent for the first $500 and 7 percent for the balance.

■ You can withdraw money that has accumulated in your cash value. If you do, your death benefit decreases because it depends partially upon the accumulated cash value.

■ You can borrow against the cash value of your policy at a fixed rate, generally below market rates.

■ If you increase your coverage, you may have to requalify by taking a medical exam.

■ You probably have to pay a termination fee or surrender charge *(backloading)*. This fee decreases each year you have the policy, but it does lower the amount of your cash value.

Table 6-1 illustrates the premiums, expenses, death benefit, cash value, and surrender value of a sample universal life insurance policy.

Table 6-1: Sample Financial Transactions and Surrender Value

End of Month	Premium	Expense Charge	Cost of Insurance	Death Benefit	Interest Credited	Ending Cash Value	Surrender Value
1	$51.07	$3.83	$27.37	$50,000	—	$7,184	$7,134
2	$51.07	$3.83	$27.36	$50,000	$39.27	$7,203	$7,153
3	$51.07	$3.83	$27.34	$50,000	$39.61	$7,262	$7,212
4	$51.07	$3.83	$27.32	$50,000	$39.94	$7,322	$7,272
5	$51.07	$3.83	$27.30	$50,000	$40.28	$7,382	$7,332
6	$51.07	$3.83	$27.29	$50,000	$40.62	$7442	$7,392
7	$51.07	$3.83	$27.27	$50,000	$40.96	$7,502	$7,452
8	$51.07	$3.83	$27.25	$50,000	$41.31	$7,563	$7,513
9	$51.07	$3.83	$27.23	$50,000	$41.66	$7,625	$7,575
10	$51.07	$3.83	$27.22	$50,000	$42.00	$7,687	$7,637
11	$51.07	$3.83	$27.20	$50,000	$42.36	$7,748	$7,698
12	$51.07	$3.83	$27.18	$50,000	$42.71	$7,811	$7,761
Total	$612.84	$45.96	$327.33	$50,000	$450.72	$7,874	$7,824

Generating Interest

Insurance companies frequently have two or more interest rates that kick in at different levels. For example, the guaranteed interest rate may be 4 percent on the first $500 and 7 percent on balances over $500. With a balance of almost $8,000, the total interest is just under 7 percent.

When you're choosing a policy or company from which to buy your universal life policy, pick the one with the highest guaranteed interest so that your cash value grows most quickly.

The interest earned continues to increase and eventually will equal and then exceed the amount you contribute. At this point, the money you pay is, in effect, going directly into your own account.

The interest rate is calculated daily, so you get *compounded interest* (interest on your interest). For a policy with an interest rate of 7 percent, the annual percentage rate (APR) is actually more than 8 percent.

Borrowing Against Your Cash Value

Universal life policies allow you to borrow against your cash value, usually at interest rates below what you can get elsewhere, even for loans secured against other assets. However, borrowing against your policy generally lowers the interest you receive on your cash value, making it equal to or less than the interest at which you borrow.

For example, say that you earn 4 percent on the first $500 of cash value and 7 percent on any amount in excess of that $500. You now have an accumulated cash value, or *surrender value,* of $7,874. You can borrow $3,000 against this policy at a 6 percent interest rate — well below what you can get at a bank (even for another type of secured loan) — so this deal is quite good if you need the cash. But the interest you earn on the cash value of the insurance policy is no longer the 7 percent of the amount over $500. In fact, the interest you earn takes into account the $3,000 you borrowed, and the total interest you earn on your account is

- 4 percent on the first $500

- 6 percent on the next $3,000 (the amount borrowed)

- 7 percent on the balance

Death Benefits Options

With universal life insurance, you can choose how much death benefit is to be paid. You have two options, and although the options appear similar, some subtle differences between them can change the amount dramatically. With both options, your premium remains the same throughout the term of the policy, but the death benefit and surrender value differ.

Option 1: Fixed death benefit

When you choose a *fixed death benefit,* whatever amount you sign up for (in the example, $50,000) goes to your survivors. In actuality, the face value of the policy — the initial $50,000 — decreases by the amount you've accumulated in your cash value account. The death benefit remains the same because the decreased face value and the increased cash value add up to the total amount you chose.

Option 2: Increasing death benefit

With the second option, your death benefit increases in line with the increase in your cash value. Your survivors get the surrender value, which certainly appears to be a great deal more for the consumer than what Option 1 provides.

So what's the catch? Why would anyone choose Option 1? With Option 2, your cash value increases more slowly than with Option 1. So you must continue paying the annual premiums, often when you no longer need the same kind of protection you did 25 years earlier.

Table 6-2 illustrates the two types of death benefit options you can choose with universal life insurance.

Which option is for me?

If you look at Table 6-2, you can see that the two death benefit options differ significantly. If you die in 25 years, your survivors receive $18,000 more under Option 2. On the other hand, if you *don't* die during that time and instead take your surrender value, you're better with Option 1. In effect, by choosing Option 1, you're gambling on a long life so that you can withdraw a larger cash value.

To determine which option is best for you, you must consider a number of factors:

- Your current age and health
- How much protection your dependents will need as you age
- Whether you can increase your net worth at a greater rate by investing in other options
- How much of a gamble you're willing to take

Table 6-2:   Fixed versus Increasing Death Benefit Universal Life Policies

End of Year	Annual Premium	Death Benefit Option 1			Death Benefit Option 2		
		Ending Cash Value	Surrender Value	Death Benefit	Ending Cash Value	Surrender Value	Death Benefit
5	$612	$1,803	$1,753	$50,000	$1,803	$1,803	$51,803
10	$612	$3,462	$3,412	$50,000	$3,262	$3,262	$53,262
15	$612	$8,322	$8,272	$50,000	$7,822	$7,822	$57,822
20	$612	$12,382	$12,332	$50,000	$11,382	$11,382	$61,382
25	$612	$19,874	$19,824	$50,000	$17,874	$17,874	$67,874

Premiums

The amounts of your death benefit, accumulated cash value, and premium are all interrelated with universal life. The more you pay per month in premiums, either the more protection you're buying or the more cash value you're building. You can't have both. The higher the protection you buy, either the higher your premiums or the lower your cash value. And the more cash value you want to build, either the higher the premium or the less protection you're buying.

Because your primary goal in buying insurance is protection, your primary consideration should be the amount of the death benefit. Cash value and your premium cost should be secondary factors, but clearly, your premium should be in line with how much you can afford to pay.

Choosing your premium

If you want a universal life policy and believe that you can afford the premium, you need to balance the following three considerations to determine your cash value:

- Determine how much you can afford from your monthly budget.

- Decide how much protection you want to purchase.

- Balance the amount of protection you want to purchase with the amount of premium you can afford.

You invest in a life insurance policy to be covered in case you die, not because life insurance is a good investment. You can generally make more money by putting your money into other investments.

Prepaying your premium

With universal life insurance, you can buy in up-front by putting a significant sum into your account, which allows your cash value to increase more because your account is starting at a higher level. Prepaying also allows you to lower your premiums because the accumulated cash value is earning more, which means that more of your earnings can contribute to the cost of the insurance. On the other hand, prepaying also means that you must take a lump sum of cash from somewhere.

Is prepaying for you? Not likely, unless you really want insurance but can't afford monthly payments. People have generally used prepaid insurance as an investment to build cash value without incurring any tax consequences. But with IRAs, Roth IRAs, and 401(k)s, chances are you won't be interested in this option.

Summing Up

Table 6-3 compares the pros and cons of universal life insurance.

Table 6-3:   Pros and Cons of Universal Life Insurance

Pros	Cons
A lot of flexibility — you can tailor the premiums, cash value, and death benefit to suit your needs.	Complicated terms and options; you have to trust your agent to guide you to the best plan for you.
Premium remains constant for the entire time you're covered, *and* you can opt for either a fixed death benefit or an increasing death benefit.	Premiums are considerably higher than for term insurance, and if your death benefit remains fixed, you actually reduce the accumulated cash value.

Continued

Table 6–3: Pros and Cons of Universal Life Insurance *(continued)*

Pros	Cons
Coverage is totally paid after only a few years by the profits from the cash value, and most of your premiums are going to you.	Whether from your monthly budget or your accumulated cash value, you're still paying the premium. Not appropriate as an investment due to poor rate of return.
Lifetime coverage and no medical exam (unless you make changes to the policy).	Death benefit coverage becomes unnecessary later in life when you have no policy). dependent beneficiaries.
Tax-deferred cash-value earnings, and when you cash out, the premiums you paid reduce the gain.	Returns aren't as high as other tax-deferred plans such as IRAs and 401(k)s (which allow you to invest your money wherever you want).

Comparing Universal Life Insurance Policies

If you've decided that universal life insurance is for you, the next step is to get quotes from at least three insurance companies and compare them. To help you, I've provided a worksheet for you to fill out. Step 2 of the worksheet asks you to find out the rating of the insurance company — see Chapter 8 for more information about ratings companies, and see the Resource Center at the back of this book for how to obtain ratings.

Universal Life Insurance Worksheet

		Company 1	Company 2	Company 3
1.	Name of company	_____	_____	_____
2.	Rating of insurance company			
	Rating from company 1	_____	_____	_____

	Rating from company 2	_____	_____	_____
	Rating from company 3	_____	_____	_____
3.	Death benefit/amount of insurance (Use the same amount for each company for easy comparison)	_____	_____	_____
4.	Death benefit if increasing policy	_____	_____	_____
5.	Annual premium	_____	_____	_____
6.	Guaranteed rate of return	_____	_____	_____
7.	Guaranteed surrender value after:			
	1st year	_____	_____	_____
	5th year	_____	_____	_____
	10th year	_____	_____	_____
8.	Dividends			
	Is there a history of dividends?	_____	_____	_____
	Annual estimated	_____	_____	_____
	Terminal estimated	_____	_____	_____
9.	Projected surrender value after: (using agent's estimated/hoped for rate of return)			
	1st year	_____	_____	_____
	5th year	_____	_____	_____
	10th year	_____	_____	_____
10.	Additional costs if higher-risk category	_____	_____	_____
11.	Special features/ options available	_____	_____	_____

CHAPTER 7

ALL THE OTHERS

IN THIS CHAPTER

- Looking at variable life insurance
- Understanding group life insurance
- Finding out about industrial life insurance
- Checking into mortgage insurance
- Exploring endowment life insurance
- Learning about various riders

In this chapter, I talk about an interesting variation on universal life, some of the different options you have with all policies, and some ways you can save money by combining with other people. I also cover *riders,* which are some of the options you can purchase.

Variable Life

A variation on whole and universal life insurance (see Chapters 5 and 6, respectively) is a *variable life insurance policy.* Under the terms of this form of insurance, you maintain a cash value from which your term insurance premiums are paid. What makes this type of policy different is that the cash value is invested in mutual funds. The amount of your death benefit is tied to the mutual fund's performance.

Variable life investments

Typically, you have the choice of investing your cash value in a common stock mutual fund, a bond fund, a money market fund, or any combination of funds. You maintain the control. With some variable life insurance policies, you can change funds, but you're always investing in the insurance company's funds. The success of these funds depends on how successful the insurance company's investment managers are.

Variable life death benefits

The amount of your death benefit with a variable life policy varies but is typically never below the face value. If your investments go up, so does your death benefit. If it decreases — well, so does your death benefit. In fact, that's one of the biggest dangers of this kind of policy.

If your investments go down, so, too, does your death benefit! And remember, you're buying life insurance *not* as an investment but to protect your survivors if you die. Consequently, some insurance professionals are wary of this type of insurance.

However, a variable life policy with a minimum guaranteed death benefit is a whole different story, at least as far as protection goes. With a guaranteed death benefit, variable life can be excellent insurance policies because if the investments are successful, the cash value can go up much more than a policy with a fixed rate of return.

Straight versus universal variable life

You can get two different kinds of variable life policies: a *straight variable policy,* in which your premium is fixed and the death benefit rises and falls as the investments go up and down, and a *variable universal policy,* in which the premiums vary, the death benefit is either fixed or increases (just like a normal universal life policy), and your cash value goes up and down with your investments.

With the straight variable, if the value of your investment exceeds a specified minimum (usually 4 percent), the death benefit goes up by that amount. If your investment's value decreases, so does your death benefit. And with most policies, your death benefit will never decrease below the original face value.

If you're considering purchasing a straight variable life insurance policy, make certain it has a guaranteed death benefit.

Other terms of variable life

Most of the other terms of variable life policies are the same as a universal life policy:

■ You can borrow against your cash value.

In many policies, the amount you borrow is limited by the amount that's invested in a money market fund, which often gets a lower rate of return than the stock or bond funds. This sort of defeats the purpose of buying this kind of policy to take advantage of the more dramatic rises in the stock market.

■ You can choose to have an increasing or fixed death benefit.

■ Your cash-value earnings are all tax-deferred, which adds value for many people.

The bottom line on variable life

For many people, variable life is an excellent product because it combines flexibility and bigger returns. But it also adds in considerably higher costs. The premiums are much higher than universal life, in part because the expense charges are much higher. Remember, your investments are paying not only for the cost of your term life insurance but *also* for the cost of the company's investment managers.

The purpose of life insurance is to protect your survivors. Although you want to choose the right kind of policy for your needs, you're not insuring yourself to make a killing on the market. So make sure that any policy you buy, especially a variable life policy, has a guaranteed death benefit. If you're looking for a good return on your money and want to invest, particularly in a tax-deferred vehicle, you're probably better off doing so through an IRA or 401(k).

Group Life

Life insurance, like any other commodity, is cheaper when you buy a lot of it (which is why $100,000 policies aren't double the price of $50,000 policies), and cheaper when a lot of people buy it. When tens, or hundreds, or thousands of people agree to purchase policies from one company, that company can offer rates considerably less than if you buy a policy on your own.

Typically, group life insurance is arranged through your employer or an organization to which you belong. One of the key things to remember about group life policies is that *you don't own the policy!* Although you're the one who is covered, the policy belongs to your employer or organization, not you. If you find a different job, retire, or quit, or you no longer are a member in the organization through which you purchased the insurance, you can no longer buy the coverage.

Be aware that you may suffer tax consequences when your employer pays for your life insurance. The premium that your employer pays for your life insurance coverage is, in effect, income. Therefore, you're responsible for paying taxes on that income. However, under the current tax rules, employers are allowed to provide up to $50,000 in term life insurance for you without your facing any tax consequence. Any premium paid for a policy above that minimum is considered additional income for which you must pay taxes. So if your employer purchases a $250,000 term life insurance policy for you, for which the company pays $850 per year (and the company can buy a $50,000 policy for $300), you must count the additional $550 as income on your tax return.

The cost of group term life insurance over $50,000 is item C in Box 13 of your annual W-2 Earnings Summary.

Industrial Life

Industrial life, also called *burial life,* is a specialized kind of policy that isn't too common. As its name implies, the policy pays a small amount to your beneficiaries for your burial expenses. The premiums are quite low because the policy's face value — the cost of burial — is fairly low. In essence, industrial life is another term life policy, but the death benefit is specifically tied to the cost of burial.

For most people, industrial/burial life insurance is *not* a good buy. It's usually more expensive than simple term insurance and doesn't pay your beneficiaries for anything other than your burial. If, however, you feel that you would like enough coverage to pay for your burial, you should speak with an agent about buying or increasing a life insurance policy.

Mortgage Insurance

Mortgage insurance is, essentially, another term insurance program designed specifically to pay the balance of your home mortgage. As you pay off your mortgage, the balance declines, and so does your mortgage insurance death benefit.

If you want enough life insurance coverage to pay for your mortgage, speak with an agent about buying or increasing a life insurance policy.

Endowment Policies

Endowment insurance policies are unique because they're both savings plans that build cash value *and* term life insurance policies that expire if you don't die. People who want the proceeds of their insurance to go to some organization, such as a college or charity, may take out endowment policies.

If you're interested in this kind of plan, talk it over with a trusted and *knowledgeable* agent. Few insurance agents know much about these plans because they're very specific and people don't use them very often. You may want to speak directly to the fundraising director of the organization you want to be the beneficiary.

Riders

Riders is the term used in the insurance business for options that you can purchase as extras. Riders are some of the most important parts of the policy. When you purchase a life insurance policy, pay special attention to the riders being offered.

Most riders cost you additional fees. But one, an *automatic premium loan,* is almost always offered to you at no charge if you have a cash-value policy (whole life or universal life) and you check off the box that requests it. With this rider, the company pays your premium from your cash value if you don't pay, either because you forget or because the payment is never received.

For most insurance policyholders, taking this rider is a smart decision. Remember, insurance is protection. Don't get caught without protection just because your check gets lost in the mail or you forget to send it in.

Family rider protection

One of the options available with cash value policies — whole life, universal life, and most variable life — is the opportunity to purchase a term life insurance policy for others in your family under your cash-value policy. This benefit usually saves you a great deal of money.

Say, for example, that you're 40 years old and you buy a universal life or whole life policy. You're building some cash value and, at the same time, using your premium to buy your term life coverage *and* add to your cash value. As the cash value grows and earns interest, either more of your premium goes toward your cash value, or the additional amount it earns goes toward paying the higher premiums for your coverage.

You may also want to cover your spouse in the event of his or her untimely death because both of you bring in income to support the family. If you go out and buy a separate term life policy for your spouse, you're probably going to pay much more than if you broaden your coverage to include the other person.

Look before you leap, and compare the numbers by using the tables provided in Chapter 10.

Generally, breadwinners use insurance to protect their family, so purchasing life insurance for your children is usually unnecessary.

Double indemnity

Double indemnity is also called *accidental death*. Essentially, this rider pays your survivors twice the amount of the policy if you die an accidental death, as opposed to death by disease or illness. Some policies offer a triple death benefit if the accident occurs while you're a passenger on a common carrier, such as a commercial airline, train, or bus.

Accidental death riders sometimes raise questions about whether a death is a result of an accident or an illness or disease. Most policies specify that in order to be covered under this rider, the insured must die within 90 days of an accident, and the cause of death must be *directly related* to the accident — and that may be hard to prove.

Although accidental death/double indemnity riders are quite cheap, for most people they're not really good deals. After all, you base how much you insure yourself for on your survivors' needs, and an accidental death won't increase the amount they need. (In fact, they probably need less than if you die from an illness, because illness often brings additional and prolonged costs.)

If this coverage appeals to you, you probably feel under insured. Instead, consider raising your amount of coverage.

Nondeath and living needs benefits

Another rider benefit that many policies (particularly newer ones) offer is a *nondeath benefit,* where the insured receives the insurance payout without dying.

One of these provisions covers accidental dismemberment, in which you lose an arm, a leg, or vision in one or both eyes due to an accident (not an illness or disease). Typically, you can receive a portion of the total face value, depending on whether you lose one limb or two, one eye or two, and so on. The insurance contract clearly spells out the amounts you receive in each instance.

You can also get a policy rider to cover you if you suffer a catastrophic illness such as a stroke or kidney disease, and a rider if you suffer from a terminally ill disease. This kind of coverage has become increasingly popular as more and more people face the issues of aging, AIDS, and high-tech medical care that extends lives.

With this rider, if you are terminally ill and have less than one year to live (your doctors must provide certified statements to that effect), your insurance company will allow you to, in effect, take an advance on the face value of your death benefit. Usually, you can withdraw a percentage of the total coverage — perhaps as much as half, although more likely one-quarter or one-third. Most companies charge a fee to take advantage of this benefit, the amount of which depends on how much coverage you have and the percentage you're withdrawing. The amount you take out reduces your death benefit, so if you live longer than expected, your coverage is lower.

Don't confuse this kind of coverage with disability insurance, which covers your expenses if you become partially or totally disabled and can't work, or long-term care insurance, which pays for nursing home care or in-home nursing care. This coverage is an actual payment from your life insurance company because you're terminally ill and you want to be able to use some of the death benefit before you die.

Cost of living adjustments

Another rider that many people feel strongly about is the cost of living rider. It works fairly simply: Each year, the amount of death benefit increases based on some neutral statistic, usually the Consumer Price Index (CPI) put out by the federal government. If you choose this rider, the face value of your insurance policy automatically increases by this percentage. For example:

> If you have a $100,000 policy and the CPI is 3 percent, the coverage goes up 3 percent, to $103,000.

> The next year, when the CPI is 2.5 percent, your coverage rises 2.5 percent, to $105,575.

Naturally, you don't get this additional benefit for free. Instead, either your premiums rise to pay for the additional coverage or, if you have a cash-value policy and your premium is constant, the insurance company reduces the amount that goes into your cash value.

One of the benefits of a cost of living rider is that your coverage goes up without your having to requalify for a higher amount. That means no new medical exams later in life when you may not qualify.

Tip

In that regard, this rider can be a pretty good deal: Your insurance coverage goes up to reflect the new needs of your survivors without your having to worry that you won't qualify for the higher amount.

On the other hand, the amount of increased coverage can be pretty small. In the last several years, for example, the inflation rate has been quite low. Adding 2 or 3 percent is not likely to make much difference to your survivors. Secondly, with most policies you get to choose each year whether to purchase the higher amount. But if you decline in any one year, you no longer have the option in later years and have to requalify if you want to buy the rider again.

If this rider appeals to you, chances are your concern is really more about the total protection you have purchased than the small yearly increases. Speak with your family, your financial advisor, and your insurance agent about these concerns. And if some event occurs in your life that warrants increasing your coverage — the birth of a child or a new job that results in a dramatic increase in the cost of your lifestyle, for example — buy a larger policy.

Guaranteed insurability

The idea that you can always buy more insurance later if you need to is very appealing to people, making the *guaranteed insurability rider* sound enticing. With this rider, you buy only what you need now, and when your situation changes later on and you need or want additional protection, you just buy more. You don't have to worry about requalifying; you just purchase a new amount at the prevailing standard rates for someone your age.

For the privilege of being able to buy more insurance later without having to requalify, you pay more now. And with most guaranteed insurability riders, you can exercise this option only until you're 45 or 50 years old (or a defined period of years, depending on the terms of your policy), which means that the additional payments you make along the way are wasted if you don't increase your coverage by then. Furthermore, this rider is only offered with cash-value policies, which already cost more.

If you decide to purchase that added protection, make sure that you know how long you have to exercise your option.

Policy protection: Waiver of premium

If you become disabled and can no longer work, you probably won't be able to pay your life insurance premium either.

By purchasing a waiver of premium rider, you ensure that your insurance isn't canceled, even though you don't pay the premiums. You usually have to wait six months from the time you become disabled before this benefit kicks in.

Read the definitions and terms in these riders carefully and discuss them with your agent. Some waivers take over the payments if you can't work in your chosen profession (or a profession in which you have experience or for which you're trained), while other waiver of premium riders pay only if you can't work in *any* job. Still others may combine these requirements so that for a period of time (two years, for example), the company waives the premium if you can't work in your normal line of work, but after that waives the premium only if you can't work in any job. The insurance company will most likely conduct its own medical exam to verify that you are disabled and unable to work.

For universal life insurance policyholders, the waiver of premium rider works a bit differently. Because a changing portion of your premium goes toward the insurance coverage and the rest for administrative fees and cash value, the waiver of premium rider only covers the cost of the insurance and the administrative fees. No additions are made to your cash-value portion except from any interest that is earned.

Buying this rider usually costs you 5 to 10 percent more, possibly higher for term life because you're always renewing it. To qualify, you must have documentation from your physician that you've become disabled and can't work.

For most life insurance holders, a waiver of premium rider is probably *not* such a good deal. You're better off increasing a disability insurance policy because it would pay for your expenses — including a life insurance premium — if you became disabled. But if you don't have disability insurance, this rider may be an inexpensive means to add that coverage without having to buy a whole new disability policy.

CHAPTER 8
BUYING LIFE INSURANCE

IN THIS CHAPTER

- Using ratings to select the right company
- Choosing the right agent
- Buying online or through the mail
- Understanding the qualifying medical exam and the high risk categories
- What to do if you fail the exam

After you find out about the different insurance products available, you need to start thinking about which product to buy and which company to buy it from. In this chapter, I guide you through the process of judging a company by the ratings, selecting an agent, and selecting the right product. I also talk about qualifying for life insurance, with particular emphasis on the medical exam and what to do if you're not in good health, you smoke, or you work in a high-risk occupation.

You have two rules to follow when choosing a life insurance policy:

Rule 1: Choose the company, not the agent.

Rule 2: Choose the insurance product, not just the company.

Selecting the Right Company

As with any product you purchase, keep the following things in mind during your search for a life insurance provider:

■ Make sure that you're selecting the right company for your needs.

■ Be certain that if you're dissatisfied, you can cancel your policy without incurring any charges.

■ Make sure that the insurance company backs up its product, even if an individual agent goes out of business.

Insurance is a unique product. You're buying the future, not the present. You have to buy the best product from a company you *know* can deliver when called upon. The whole point of insurance is *protection for your survivors.* The product doesn't even come into being until you die. So when you're selecting a company from which to buy the product, do what you can to make certain the company will be around to pay off.

Checking into a company's ratings

Five major independent insurance ratings companies analyze almost all the insurance companies (you can find their contact information in the Resource Center at the back of this book):

■ A.M. Best Company

■ Duff & Phelps Credit Rating Co.

■ Moody's Investors Service

■ Standard & Poor's Insurance Rating Services

■ Weiss Research

Each of these ratings services has its strong and weak points, and the ratings are not all consistent. But they all do basically the same thing:

■ Analyze the financial strength of insurance companies

■ Evaluate the stability of insurance companies

■ Make judgments about the reliability of insurance companies

Most professionals feel strongly that you should *not* purchase a life insurance policy from a company until you check out its rating.

When selecting an insurance company, get the ratings on several from at least two ratings companies. The ratings systems vary: An A from Weiss, for example, is the second-best rating a company can receive. Only an A+ is better. But an A from Standard & Poor's is much farther down the list. It's sixth, behind AAA, AA+, AA, AA-, and A+. Quite a difference.

Even if you can equate the scales, the ratings of the ratings companies differ from one another. For example, Best may offer an insurance company its top rating (AAA), while Moody's gives the company its fourth-highest rating (Aa3). So how can you judge?

You can check *Consumer Reports* magazine. The magazine evaluates the different life insurance companies and uses a rating system that averages all the other systems to make its determinations. You can get a copy of *Consumer Reports* at your local library or check its Web site at www.consumer-reports.com. (See the Resource Center at the back of this book for more great Web sites.)

What if the company goes belly-up?

If a company *does* fail, chances are good that your protection will be honored. The insurance regulators (state and federal agencies) work with other companies to pick up the policies from a failed company. If that effort fails, your policy may be picked up by a *guaranty association,* a state association made up of all the insurers in your state who collectively ensure that you won't be left in the lurch.

Although these backups are comforting, if your state association picks up your policy because no other insurance company will, you may lose some of your benefits. Most state guaranty associations have limits on the death benefit (generally not more than $500,000), and they also may not match the interest you're guaranteed on a cash-value policy. Check with your state insurance commission for more information about insurance company bankruptcies.

The best thing you can do to make sure you don't lose your investment or your protection is to choose your life insurance company wisely.

Selecting the Right Agent

Many insurance "stores" carry a number of different "brands" of insurance. These kinds of insurance stores or sales agents act as *independent brokers,* bringing you, the customer, together with the insurance company.

In this case, you choose the agent before you choose the insurance company. This method seems to go against Rule 1, but actually, you haven't yet chosen the company. You've chosen an agent to present you with options. Hopefully, that agent will present you with products from more than one company, allowing you to choose both the right product and the right company.

If the agent can present you with only one company, rethink your position and consider the first rule: Choose the company, not the agent.

Many insurance agents think of themselves as counselors as well as sales agents. They have a variety of products to sell, one of which you're interested in buying. The agent's job is to help you decide which one.

Your insurance sales agent is a knowledgeable resource for you who can serve as a counselor, helping you decide which product is best for you. Therefore, you need to find someone you trust. Through an open dialogue, your agent should be able to steer you to the right product.

Beware of high-pressure tactics. Although most sales agents are honest, you may run across a slick, hard-sell insurance salesperson who only wants to sell you something without due concern for your needs or your budget. Check with others who use a prospective agent, and make sure that he or she is a registered member of the National Association of Life Underwriters (NALU) or the Society of Financial Service Professionals (see the Resource Center for contact information).

Shopping for Insurance Online

As more and more products become available through the Internet, more and more people are shopping for insurance online. Hundreds, or perhaps thousands, of Web sites are devoted to insurance, with more springing up every day. At the time of this writing, a search for "life insurance," using one of the large search engines (`www.excite.com`) revealed thousands of matches. A review of just ten of these matches, selected almost at random, showed that most can lead you to a company from which you can buy life insurance. (For more great Web sites, see the Resource Center at the back of this book.)

Is shopping online a good idea? Take a look at the pluses and minuses in Table 8-1 and then make your determination.

Table 8-1: Pluses and Minuses of Shopping Online

Pluses	Minuses
You can choose from a huge number of companies.	You're on your own, which means you can't rely on getting guidance or counseling from a human being.
You can do all the research imaginable on a company without leaving your computer.	You don't develop a relationship with the online insurance company representatives or know anything about their experience.
You generally pay lower prices by buying online than from an insurance "store."	Your search for a product is only as good as the search engine(s) you use.
You can choose from a vast range of products.	The amount of information can be overwhelming and too time-intensive to weed through.
You have the tools to shop around for the best company that offers the best product at the best price.	You have to know exactly what you want and need because you won't have an agent who knows your family, your total portfolio, or your goals — important elements in selecting the right life insurance product.

Follow these steps to make your decision on which online company to buy your life insurance from:

1. Do all the shopping and research you can online.

2. Narrow your search to the top two or three policies and companies.

3. Call and solicit recommendations and advice from the online and telephone assistants (if that option is available). Or use e-mail to correspond.

4. Collect all the hard facts about the policy, the company, and the company ratings from the independent ratings companies.

5. If the company has both online and agent service, call and make an appointment to meet or talk with a company representative. Have that representative give you guidance, counseling, and a quote.

6. From friends and relatives, get the name of an insurance agent who doesn't represent an online insurance company.

7. Talk to that agent and have him or her give you guidance, counseling, and a quote. Assuming you feel that the online companies are all good ones, give the agent a chance to match or beat your online offer.

8. Make your decision.

Buying through the Mail

Most professionals frown on buying life insurance from a direct-mail flyer sent out to you and thousands of your closest friends promising you personal service. Although buying a life insurance policy through the mail may have been a decent alternative a few years ago, today it pales when compared to the positives of buying online.

But if a flyer sparks your interest, consider it just as much as you would an insurance policy you discover through an online search. Do your homework. Compare terms, rates, company ratings, and talk with a trusted agent (or a recommended agent) to see whether the company is legitimate. Make sure that you can actually talk with someone at the company itself.

Like most things, if it sounds too good to be true, it probably is.

Qualifying for the Coverage You Want

The concept of life insurance is simple: Although you hope you live a long life, you also pay a company to make sure that if you die sooner rather than later, your survivors have something to fall back on. The company, similarly, is hoping that you don't die before it has a chance to make more on what you pay than the cost of paying your survivors. You know that you will die eventually — the only question is when. Your only gamble is which insurance company you choose.

But companies don't like to gamble, so they stack the deck. The more likely you are to die sooner rather than later, the more the company needs to get from you in the early years of your policy. If, on the other hand, the company can count on you being around for a long time, it doesn't need as much each month to make a profit from your premiums.

So how does the company make this judgment? It uses the answers to two questions:

- Based on complicated statistical analyses and longevity charts, how long are you likely to live?

- Based on your medical history and information, are you a high or low risk?

The company then bases your premiums on the answers to those questions. If you're too old or too unhealthy, the company doesn't want to insure you because it will probably have to pay off before it can make a profit from your premiums (or it'll charge you so much that the cost won't be worth the coverage to you).

To qualify for a life insurance policy, you have to pass two conditions: You have to be young enough, and you have to be healthy enough.

The age condition is based strictly on statistics gathered for large numbers of people. If you're older than 60 or 65, most companies won't insure you. If you're younger than that, the company will insure you, basing your premiums on your age.

To judge your medical condition, the company will ask you to provide your complete medical history and, for most policies, will ask you to undergo a medical exam.

Taking the medical exam

Medical exams for life insurance can involve anything from a quick review of your medical history, your family's medical history, noting your height and weight, and taking basic vital signs (blood pressure and pulse) and a swab of cells from the inside of your cheek, or it can be a more extensive exam requiring an EKG (electrocardiogram), blood tests, X-rays, and urinalysis. In addition, on your insurance application, you give the insurance company permission to check with your doctor to follow up on any findings or questionable items on the application.

The extent of your physical exam is based on the following:

■ Your age

■ Your medical history

■ Your family's medical history

■ Whether you smoke

■ The amount of insurance you're seeking to buy

For the quick review, usually a health professional comes to your home or office. If you need to undergo more testing, the company may ask you to see a physician or go to a clinic. The insurance company bears the cost of the exam (although, of course, such administrative costs are built into the cost of the insurance policy you purchase).

What "high risk" means

Insurance companies are concerned about a number of high-risk people:

- Smokers

- People with high cholesterol

- Potential diabetics

- People with indications of coronary disease

- People with a personal history of cancer or other serious disease

- People who work in high-risk occupations

If you fall into one or more of these categories, you face three possible outcomes:

- The company won't insure you.

- The company will charge you a higher premium.

- The company will ignore the high risk (which isn't likely).

What if I fail the exam?

If the company refuses to insure you because of your medical condition, first check that the medical report is accurate. Request that the company send a copy either to you (which they may not do) or to your doctor (which they will do). Go over the report with your doctor. You may be facing legitimate health concerns that you need to address.

If you find a mistake on your medical report, notify the insurance company in writing immediately. Being turned down for life insurance can affect other insurance applications that you may be filing.

If the medical report is correct and the company charges you a higher premium, appeal to the agent who sold you the policy, although chances are you'll have very little luck changing the amount. You can go to a different company, but they're likely to discover the same problems and raise their premium as well. At that point, you either pay the higher premium or lower the face value to lower the premium. You can also try to find an insurance policy that doesn't require a medical exam or that requires only a limited exam. (An independent agent may be able to refer you to another company.) In any case, discuss the situation with your agent to see whether the two of you can come up with a solution.

CHAPTER 9
HOW MUCH SHOULD YOU PAY?

IN THIS CHAPTER

- Calculating premiums
- Dealing with mortality charges
- Understanding underwriting
- Comparing rates and companies

Insurance companies use formulas to determine how much risk you pose and weigh that against how much profit they can make. This chapter illustrates how insurance companies calculate their premiums, tells you about the factors that affect your rate, and points out some of the hidden charges you need to know about. The chapter concludes by explaining the basics of how to compare one company's policy with another's.

How Premiums Are Calculated

Before you can determine whether a premium is reasonable, you have to know how insurance companies determine the cost. So many of the costs are hidden inside the cash value, projected earnings, and dividends that figuring out how much you're actually paying isn't as easy as it sounds, even with term insurance. You know how much goes out of your checking account each month for the policy. And you know at the end of each year how much the surrender value is, if you have a cash-value policy. Theoretically, you can just subtract the amount in your account from the amount you paid out. But what about next year? What about cancellation charges? The next sections take you through the basics.

The costs of term insurance

Every year (or every month or quarter or semiannually), you pay a set premium for term insurance, which covers you for that period. The next period, you pay again, either the same amount or a higher amount. Whether the amount is higher depends on whether you buy a one-year term, a five-year term, or another multiple-year policy.

If you have a one-year term policy, you pay the one year and the company raises the premium each year. You don't know how much you'll pay next year. With a one-year term policy, you don't know how much you'll pay three or four years from now. Most companies can give you a pretty good estimate (provided that you select a company that has a proven track record of estimating accurately). But the key is whether the company provides dividends. If your premium is $346 per year and the dividend is $183, you pay just $163. If you buy a five-year term policy, the company declares the $183 dividend for all five years and you pay the same $163 each year. If you choose to renew for another five years, you pay the next premium minus the dividend rate for five more years (refer to Chapter 3 for more information on dividends and to Chapter 4 for a discussion of term insurance).

With multiple-year policies like a five-year term, the company figures the premium based on the middle year. So if you're 38 years old and buy a five-year term policy, the insurance company charges the same premium for all five years; it bases the premium on your age as though you were 41 for all five years (plus a slight, built-in inflation factor).

If you add any options (convertibility, for example — see Chapter 7), the premium may go up slightly. On the other hand, if you choose a decreasing term policy, such as mortgage insurance, in which the death benefit decreases, your premium remains the same.

The costs of cash-value insurance

Term insurance is simple. Cash-value, as you may have guessed, isn't so simple. Cash-value is also much more expensive because you're paying not only for the protection, administrative fees, and commissions, but also to build up the investment so that the interest it generates will pay the costs of the protection, fees, and commissions. In addition, you're paying more for the flexibility a cash-value policy gives you.

The one thing that's simple about cash-value policies is that the premium remains the same for the entire time.

So what changes? Well, everything else, including, in many cases, the amount that goes to your survivors.

When you purchase a cash-value policy, you pay a set premium based on the amount of protection you're buying, the amount needed to pay the insurance company's other costs, and the guaranteed amount that will accrue in your account. How all those numbers are configured is an extremely complex formula based on amortization tables, actuarial mortality charts, and contracts with life insurance salespeople.

Unless you have a burning desire to wade through the numbers, the only things you really have to be concerned with are

- How much protection you're buying (so that the death benefit is sufficient for your needs)

- The amount of your total premium (to be sure that you can afford the monthly payment)

- The guaranteed return (so you know how much will go into your investment)

Mortality Charges

When you pare things down to the bare essentials, life insurance is about how much you have to pay to insure your loved ones. The insurance company determines your rate as follows:

1. The insurance company and the industry at-large keep statistics on the mortality rates throughout the country, based on its own research or by relying on research done by others, such as the National Association of Insurance Commissioners. Through this research, the insurance company knows how many men and women in various age ranges (for example, 25- to 29-year-olds, 30- to 34-year-olds, 35- to 39-year-olds, and so on) die each year.

2. The insurance company uses these numbers and some others to determine your life expectancy.

3. The insurance company then calculates how much money it has to earn on your premiums so that when it pays your survivors, it pays less than what it has made.

Does that mean that if you have a $50,000 death benefit you will have paid more than $50,000? No. Definitely not. In fact, chances are with a term policy you'll have paid no more than half to two-thirds of that figure, depending on your age when you die. Keep in mind that the insurance company makes money on the premiums you pay. Many other policyholders continue to pay premiums, and the company uses these premiums to pay out death benefits. Many people pay premiums for years but stop their insurance before they die, and the company gets to keep all that money.

4. The insurance company builds in the commission it pays the agent who sold you the policy.

5. The insurance company adds in the other costs of doing business, such as overhead, administrative costs, salaries, employee benefits, and a profit. Even mail-order or online policies involve some costs of doing business.

6. The insurance company totals all these numbers, which is the mortality charge.

Your agent, if you use one, should be able to tell you the exact amount you're being charged as a mortality charge. This amount increases with age because it's based on your life expectancy.

Underwriting

Underwriting — the process by which the insurance company determines whether or not it will insure you — is the very heart of insurance. And if you're deemed insurable, underwriting is the process by which they determine how much to charge you for the protection.

When determining whether or not you're insurable and what your premium will be, the insurance company places you into one of three categories of risk, although you do have some flexibility to negotiate a better placement. The three levels are:

■ Preferred risk

■ Standard risk

■ Substandard risk

Ideally, you want to fall into the top category. The insurance company looks at four things to determine your category of risk:

■ **Your current health status:** Through a medical history and the required medical exam, the insurance company places you into one of the categories. A personal history of illness puts you into a high-risk category. If your health has been good, you qualify at a higher level, which translates into lower premiums.

The insurance company also asks about your family's medical history, including the ages at which your parents, grandparents, and/or siblings died. If your parents died at relatively young ages or if one or both of them had serious diseases such as cancer, heart disease, or diabetes, you may fall into a higher risk category.

■ **Your projected health status:** Your current health status, your personal medical history, and your family's medical history (see the preceding bullet) all indicate how much risk you have of dying earlier than the statistics project based on your current age. Because the insurance company is betting that you'll live longer than expected, a good projection means that you'll either pay your premiums for a longer period or you'll cancel your insurance at some point. Either way, the company has use of that money and never has to pay off.

■ **Your job:** Some jobs are simply riskier than others. The degree to which your occupation places you into a high-risk category (not too many do, by the way), translates into the amount of your premium. Changing jobs or careers isn't an option for most people, and doing so just to save money on a life insurance premium is absurd. Nevertheless, you should know that your job does have an effect.

■ **Special circumstances:** If the insurance company identifies any unusual or special circumstances, it will investigate. If, for example, you suddenly — with no apparent reason — buy a $5 million policy when you're in your 20s, the insurance company may ask a few more questions than usual. Likewise, if you make a statement in your application that conflicts with other statements. If the company isn't satisfied with your answers, the underwriter will ask you to elaborate. And in some cases, the insurance company may even hire investigators who will ask questions of family members, neighbors, and friends. The degree to which you can resolve any unusual circumstances without having to force an investigation makes you more insurable at a lower premium rate.

Comparing Rates and Companies

Chapter 8 discusses how to choose the company from which you buy your life insurance policy. This section gives you steps you can use to help you get to the bottom line.

Remember

Comparing the prices of term insurance versus cash-value policies is virtually impossible.

When you're ready to start shopping for life insurance, do the following:

■ **Decide which kind of insurance:** The first thing you must do is decide *which* kind of policy you want (if you could afford it): term, whole life, universal life, or variable life. You must also decide which riders, if any, you want. Review the information in the previous chapters, which explain the details of each kind of policy and rider and goes over the pluses and minuses of each.

■ **Look for insurance companies:** Seek out at least five or six companies and/or agents who sell the kind of policy you want. Use the information in Chapter 8 to help you rate the insurance companies. Eliminate any companies that you have doubts about. If you speak with any independent agents, remember to find out which company would be underwriting your insurance.

- **Ask for quotes from each of those remaining companies or agents:** Be certain that each quote represents the same amount of death benefit with all the same riders/options you want. If possible, ask the agent or company to break down the charges so you can more easily compare the policies — which is particularly important when you evaluate cash-value policies.

If you're unsure as to which kind of policy to buy, get quotes for all the kinds of policies. Only then can you accurately decide which one is best for you.

Keys to comparing term insurance policies

To compare policies and riders by using the Term Insurance Worksheet in Chapter 4, remember these four keys:

- **The premium for the first year does not necessarily reflect the total cost of the insurance:** Many companies discount the initial premiums in order to get your business, but the total cost over a long period is higher than from other companies. If you plan to remain insured for 20 or 30 years, be sure to include the projected premiums for the next three or four terms (*terms, not years*).

- **If the company offers dividends, find out the history of the dividends so that you can reasonably rely on the projections.**

- **Compare the same categories of risk:** If one company quotes you a preferred rate while another company quotes you the standard rate, you're not necessarily comparing the rates. On the other hand, if the companies *will* actually differ in the category of risk, using the quote they will actually offer is essential.

■ **Compare the term insurance costs with the cash-value insurance costs:** If you think you may want to buy a cash-value policy in the future, you may get a better rate when converting with the same insurance company than buying a new policy.

Keys to comparing whole life insurance policies

To compare policies and riders by using the Whole Life Worksheet in Chapter 5, remember these seven keys:

■ **Premiums remain constant for the entire policy:** To compare costs and prices, you must compare the mortality charges, cash values, dividends, and death benefits.

■ **Although one company may pay a dividend while another may not, the dividend-paying company is not necessarily the better buy:** You can tell only after you get quotes.

Warning

■ **Take the projected cash-value earnings with a grain of salt:** Companies often show you charts featuring high projected returns. Use the *guaranteed return* for your comparisons.

Because earnings on whole life policies are tax-deferred, you must consider your after-tax return, not just the return itself when comparing the return on your policy to a return on a taxable investment. To calculate the after-tax return, you have to know your marginal tax rate (including your state income tax if applicable). If you're in the 28 percent federal income tax bracket and the 7 percent state income tax bracket, that means that 28 + 7, or 35 percent of a taxable return on investment will be paid to the governments. By subtracting the total tax paid from the total return, you get your after-tax return. So a 10 percent taxable return actually is the same as a

6.5 percent untaxed return (35 percent of 10 is 3.5, which, when subtracted from 10, leaves 6.5).

■ **Put extra stock into the insurance company's rating:** With term insurance, you're only concerned that the company remains solvent during the term you purchase, but with whole life, you're buying into the company itself. A company with a significantly lower rating may guarantee a slightly higher return, but you may want to seriously consider the lower-yielding but higher-rated company for your own peace of mind.

■ **Insurance is protection, not investment:** If you want to purchase a whole life policy because you think it's a good investment, think again. Many other investments such as IRAs and 401(k)s can give you a better — and still tax-deferred — return on your dollar. You may be just as well off investing your money in another tax-deferred vehicle and purchasing a lower-cost term insurance policy.

■ **Find out what happens if you terminate your coverage:** Some insurance companies have cancellation or termination charges, while others build in administrative charges up front. Include these charges into your comparisons.

Keys to comparing universal life insurance policies

Universal life insurance is similar to whole life; however, a number of differences make universal life policies more difficult to compare with each other. To compare policies and riders by using the Universal Life Worksheet in Chapter 6, remember these four keys (**Note:** You can use these same keys when comparing variable life insurance policies):

- **Premiums for universal life don't necessarily remain constant for the entire policy (unlike whole life):** Therefore, to compare costs and prices, you have to use the same premium.

- **The death benefit in a universal life policy can either remain constant or increase as your cash value increases:** Use the same death benefit option with each policy to compare costs and prices with other companies and policies.

- **Insurance companies will show you both guaranteed and hopeful projected earnings:** Take these hopeful projections with a grain of salt. Use the guaranteed earnings, and if you get more, consider it a bonus. On the other hand, you can also use the company's historical payback to get an idea of whether the hopeful projections are pie-in-the-sky or reasonably accurate.

- **Put extra stock into the insurance company's rating:** With universal and whole life, you're buying into the company itself. If one company guarantees a little more but has a significantly lower rating, you may want to seriously consider the lower-yielding but better-rated company.

- **Insurance is protection, not investment:** Many other investments can give you a better return on your dollar than universal life insurance, including IRAs and 401(k)s, both of which offer the same tax-deferred benefit. You may be just as well off putting money in other tax-deferred investments and purchasing a lower-cost term insurance policy.

CHAPTER 10

LIFE INSURANCE PROVISIONS AND OPTIONS

- ■ Determining your death benefit payment options
- ■ Reading the fine print for provisions and exclusions
- ■ Terminating your policy
- ■ Filing a claim

This chapter discusses some of the main articles in a typical life insurance contract and highlights some of the key elements that you should look for. This chapter also covers the settlement options that are available to your beneficiaries, provides sample benefit tables for life income benefits, and details how to file a claim.

Remember

Follow this basic rule: Don't sign anything that you don't understand!

Ownership

Your insurance policy is property, and you own it. The policy is real and has value, even if you have a term life insurance policy. That means that you have certain rights associated with ownership. Among these are

- ■ **The right to choose your beneficiaries:** As owner of the insurance policy, you get to decide who is the beneficiary when you die. You can change the benefici-ary, assuming that you face no other legal restrictions, such as divorce agreements in which your dependent children are specifically named as beneficiaries.

■ **The right to cancel your policy:** If you choose, you can cancel your policy at any point, either through written notice or by ceasing to make premium payments. You should note, however, that with some cash-value poli-cies, any surrender value goes toward paying the pre-mium (see Chapters 5 and 6). In addition, you may be required to pay cancellation charges.

■ **The right to convert your policy, assuming you buy that right as a rider:** If you buy a term life insurance policy but include a rider that allows you to convert to a cash-value policy at a later date without any additional qualifying, you can opt for this conversion at your dis-cretion. **Note:** If you increase the death benefit or face value, the company may require you to undergo a new medical exam and requalify, which defeats the whole purpose of buying the conversion rider.

■ **The right to cash in your surrender value at any time:** Just as you have the right to cancel your policy, you have the right to take out whatever cash value you accrue, minus any cancellation charges or administrative fees.

■ **The right to exercise any options that your policy includes:** If you include any riders or options in your policy, you can mandate how and when these options are exercised. With death benefit payments, however, your best bet may be to leave as many options open for your survivors as possible so that they can use the death ben-efit to suit their needs.

Death Benefit Payment Options

Most people assume that when a person who has life insurance dies, the beneficiaries automatically get a check in the mail as payment on the insured person's death benefit. Nothing can be further from the truth. The insurance company must be notified that one of its policyholders has died; usually, that notification must be in the form of certified copy of a legal death certificate with an embossed seal. See "Filing a Claim," later in this chapter, for more information.

Although executors of estates usually take care of these matters, that's not always the case. So if your loved one dies and you know that he or she has an active insurance policy, be sure to follow up so that the beneficiary can receive the benefit. If you need to get official copies of the death certificate, you can usually get copies for a small charge from the funeral home or whomever handled the burial or cremation.

Taking a lump-sum payment

The lump-sum payment is the most common, but death benefits are paid to beneficiaries in other ways, too.

Choosing installment payments

As the life insurance policyholder, you can designate that your beneficiary is to be paid the death benefit a little at a time, over a period of years. You can decide whether you want to designate a specific time period for these payments or that a specific amount be paid in each payment until the total death benefit runs out. Any monies that haven't yet been paid generate interest. In most instances, this income is not taxable to the beneficiary, although you and your beneficiary should certainly check with a tax advisor before making that assumption.

Maintaining the principal: Interest-only payments

You can specify that your beneficiary get a periodic payment of the interest on the death benefit's cash value. Because the beneficiary earns interest on the account, he or she must claim the benefit as taxable income. An interest-only payment option is a means of budgeting the funds while maintaining the investment. Beneficiaries usually have the option of withdrawing the principal (although generally not all at once), which defeats the purpose of this payment option. Or they can borrow against the principal by using it as collateral and get a better rate than they can get from a bank loan. Usually, the life insurance contract specifies a minimum interest rate.

Making it last: Payments for life

Another payment option is a payment-for-life program. As in the interest-only option, your beneficiary gets a periodic payment from the death benefit, which is a means of budgeting the funds while maintaining an investment. However, the amount the beneficiary receives is based on the terms you set up, the total amount of the death benefit and cash value, and the length of time you specify for the payments. With this option, the beneficiary can't withdraw the funds but is guaranteed a payment for a specified period of time or for his or her lifetime.

Table 10-1 is a sample Life Income Table that specifies the minimum amount your beneficiary will receive each month if you and your beneficiary opt for this method of payment. Note that the amount is based on the beneficiary's age and sex and whether you specify a number of years of payment or whether you leave the number of years open.

As long as the beneficiary is alive, he or she receives equal payments at the end of each monthly interval. If you choose a specific time period, then payments continue as long as the beneficiary lives or to the end of the certain period, whichever is longer. If the beneficiary dies during the specified period, that person's heirs get a lump sum payment of any balance owed.

Joining together: Joint life income

This plan uses a schedule of payments that combines the two beneficiaries' ages and sexes. The beneficiary receives payments as long as one of the two payees is alive. You can see an example in Table 10-2.

Setting up special options

If you want to set up any other kind of payment option, that's up to you and the insurance company. As long as whatever arrangements you want to make are legal, companies are usually willing to set them up. However, more than likely, they will charge a bit more for this creative arrangement because they may have to do some legal work.

As a rule, insurance professionals don't recommend that you make up your own payment options unless you have an attorney review them. The insurance and tax laws include many nuances (and, of course, they're constantly being revised); you can easily designate a creative payment program without realizing that you've created more obstacles for your beneficiaries than you want to. Many attorneys are quite familiar with other ways to designate how your heirs receive your death benefits.

Table 10-1: Life Income Table: Monthly Payments per $1,000 in Life Insurance

| Age Last Birthday | Male | Female | Life with 5 Years Certain | | Life with 10 Years Certain | | Life with 20 Years Certain | |
			Male	Female	Male	Female	Male	Female
50	$4.85	$4.53	$4.83	$4.51	$4.77	$4.48	$4.54	$4.33
55	5.36	4.94	5.32	4.92	5.32	4.85	4.84	4.60
60	6.02	5.48	5.95	5.43	5.77	5.32	5.15	4.90
65	6.92	6.18	6.80	6.10	6.46	5.90	5.43	5.20
70	8.22	7.15	7.96	7.00	7.30	6.62	5.63	5.47
75	10.10	8.54	9.52	8.24	8.20	7.47	5.74	5.66

Table 10-2: Joint Life Income Table: Monthly Payments per $1,000 in Life Insurance

Age Last Birthday	Male Female	50 54	55 59	60 64	65 69	70 74	75 79	80 84	85 & over 89 &over
Male	**Female**								
50	54	$4.19	4.33	4.47	4.58	4.67	4.74	4.79	4.82
55	59	4.33	4.53	4.72	4.90	5.04	5.16	5.24	5.29
60	64	4.47	4.72	4.99	5.25	5.48	5.67	5.81	5.90
65	69	4.58	4.90	5.25	5.61	5.97	6.29	6.53	6.71
70	74	4.67	5.04	5.48	5.97	6.50	7.01	7.44	7.78
75	79	4.74	5.16	5.67	6.29	7.01	7.78	8.52	9.15
80	84	4.79	5.24	5.81	6.53	7.44	8.52	9.70	10.83
85+	89+	4.82	5.29	5.90	6.71	7.78	9.15	10.83	12.71

Provisions and Exclusions

Every insurance contract has — usually in small print — a number of paragraphs that are essential for you to read. Basically, in addition to some fairly obvious concepts (such as, "all amounts paid will be in United States dollars"), these paragraphs list all the reasons you would *not* be covered — that is, reasons your beneficiaries would not get any of the funds you specifically provided for them.

Age and sex

This provision is a way for the insurance company to cover itself in the event that it (or you) made a mistake, listing you either as the wrong sex or as older or younger than you were at the time of application. The insurance company cites these two factors because they're the two critical elements in how much it charges you for the protection. The insurance company adjusts the policy benefits for the correct age or sex.

Suicide

Just about every life insurance application contains a suicide provision. This provision doesn't exclude all benefits if you commit suicide. Rather, it specifies that if you die as a result of suicide *within two years from the issue date of the policy,* your beneficiaries are *not* eligible for the death benefit (which may be referred to as the *Amount of Basic Plan*).

In addition, most policies also specify that if you *do* commit suicide within the two-year period, your beneficiaries will receive an amount equal to the premiums you paid on the policy from the starting date, called *date of issuance,* to the date of death by suicide.

Also note that the *waiver of premium benefit,* specifying that premiums will be waived if you become totally disabled, does *not* go into effect if the total disability results from "an intended self-injury."

War

Although some policies specifically exclude paying death benefits when you die from injuries sustained during a war — whether you belong to the military or not — many policies do not. On the other hand, policies often exclude the waiver of premium benefit if you become totally disabled as a result of war.

Non-commercial aviation

Many policies will exclude a death benefit if you die as a result of a noncommercial airplane crash, meaning an airplane ride for which no fares are required.

Dangerous activities

If you die while engaging in an inherently dangerous activity, such as skydiving or hang gliding, your policy may not cover you. Check the fine print to be certain — some policies don't exclude the activity but do charge higher premiums if you admit that you participate in these types of activities.

Incontestability clause

A key provision in most life insurance policies is the *incontestability clause.* This provision states that except for nonpayment of premiums, the company will *not* contest either the policy or the waiver of premium clause after the policy has been in force for a specified period, usually two years. So if the company discovers an error in your application after that period, it can't go back and void your policy. This provision covers you even if you misrepresent yourself on your application, unless you misrepresent your age or gender, as discussed earlier in this chapter.

Premium provisions

The policy must specify how the premiums are payable and when they are due. The policy also must specify whether you have a grace period and, if so, how long the period lasts. During the grace period, the insurance company usually extends your coverage. If you don't pay your premium by the end of the grace period, the insurance company will first look to any dividends it owes you to cover the cost of the premium. If you don't have any dividend or if the dividend is insufficient, the policy lapses and your coverage ceases. You remain covered until the insurance is officially terminated.

Next, the policy states whether any cash value will be used to pay the premium and, if so, how you will be notified.

Finally, the policy states how long you have to apply for reinstatement if your policy lapses. This period can be as long as five years after the policy lapses, although you will probably have to show proof that you're still insurable. Furthermore, you will have to pay all the unpaid premiums *plus* compounded interest, as specified in the policy contract (approximately 6 percent per year).

Termination

As the word *termination* implies, the policy states when the death benefit, all riders, and the waiver of premium benefit will end.

Because most policies have a specified age limit after which you are no longer insured, take special note of the termination clause and when the policy terminates. Doing so is especially important if you have a cash-value policy with a declining death benefit and you plan on taking out the surrender value. Toward the end of the insurance contract, as you age, the cost of the coverage becomes higher, eating more of the premium and surrender value. So be sure to withdraw the funds if you no longer want the coverage and would prefer to have the accrued value.

Filing a Claim

When a loved one dies, thinking about the life insurance policy may seem crass. Yet, ironically, thinking about life insurance can provide an enormous amount of relief. A loved one's death brings many things to think about and many expenses that are unplanned and, often, unaffordable. The cost of the funeral itself averages $5,000 to $10,000 and can be much more, and along with that expense (and others) comes the immediate loss of income.

The good news here is that filing a life insurance claim is very easy, even if you don't have all the details about the policy. In fact, it's easy even if you don't have the actual policy!

Steps to filing a claim

Here's how to file a life insurance policy claim:

1. Look around to see whether you can find the written policy.

2. Call the insurance agent who sold your loved one the policy. If no agent is listed or you don't know who the agent is, call the company itself (or *any* local agent for the company, who will either get you to the appropriate claims agent or handle it herself).

3. Fill out the papers and forms as instructed. The insurance agent can usually do most of this task for you, but the forms should be fairly simple, especially if you have the policy itself available.

4. Get a certified copy of the death certificate.

5. Submit the claim form with the death certificate. In just a matter of a few days to a week or two, you receive your settlement.

Choosing among settlement options

The most difficult part of the claim process is deciding on the settlement option you want if the policyholder hasn't already specified the payment plan. You can usually choose from several options.

Take special note of these two things:

■ You can arrange to have the funeral expenses paid directly from the proceeds of your insurance policy. The funeral director will arrange for this payment.

■ If you know your loved one was insured but you don't have the policy or know the name of the insurance company that issued the policy, you may be able to get the necessary information by contacting the American Council of Life Insurance at 1001 Pennsylvania Ave. NW, Washington, DC 20004. The Council will forward your inquiry to about 100 of the largest insurance companies in the country so that they can investigate whether your loved one had a policy with them.

CLIFFSNOTES REVIEW

Use this CliffsNotes Review to practice what you've learned in this book and to build your confidence in doing the job right the first time. After you work through the review questions and the problem-solving scenarios, you're well on your way to achieving your goal of figuring out what your life insurance needs are.

Q&A

1. True or false: Older folks usually need less life insurance because their children are grown and no longer dependent on them.

2. You should base how much life insurance you buy on all of the following EXCEPT:

   a. Your income

   b. Your assets

   c. Your cost of living

   d. Your future expenses

   e. Your age

3. Variable life insurance is similar to universal life insurance. The major difference between the two is that with variable life ___

   _____

4. What are the two basic rules to follow when selecting a life insurance company? _____

   _____

5. Estate planning consists of all of the following EXCEPT:

   a. Irrevocable trusts

   b. Powers of attorney

   c. Health care proxy

   d. Will

6. The option to buy term life insurance for your spouse under your cash-value insurance policy is called _____

7. True or False: One of the benefits of universal life insurance is that you pay less because as your need for protection decreases with age, the death benefit decreases.

8. The premium you pay for life insurance is based on:

   a. Your age

   b. Your sex

   c. Your health status

   d. Your father's health

   e. All of the above

   Answers: (1) False. (2) b. (3) Your cash value account is invested in mutual funds. (4) Choose the company, not the agent; choose the policy, not just the company (5) c. (6) Family rider protection. (7) False. (8) e.

Scenarios

1. You're in the 28 percent federal tax bracket and the 3½ percent state tax bracket. The rate of return you're getting from the money you currently have in a taxable certificate of deposit is 5 percent. The equivalent rate of return in an untaxed, life insurance cash-value account is _____

_____

2. You are single with two children whom you have designated as your life insurance beneficiaries. Your children are 12 and 9 years old. What should you do to make sure that they get the death benefit if you die prematurely?

_____

_____

3. You are single, just turned 30 years old, and have no children. Two months ago you purchased a condo for $98,000 and owe $80,000 on it. The down payment practically depleted your savings, although you still own some stock worth about $6,000. You're paying $269 per month for your car (which is worth about $8,000), and you still owe about $4,000 on it. You have no other debts and pay off your credit cards each month. You checked with an online life insurance company and found out that a $100,000 term life insurance policy would cost you about $120 per year. Is this a good investment for you? Why or why not?

_____

_____

_____

_____

_____

Answers: (1) 31.5 percent of 5.0 = 1.58; 5.0 – 1.58 = 3.42 percent. (2) Appoint a trustee because minors can't collect life insurance benefits. (3) Probably not. You have no debts except your car, which you pay off by its value, and the condo won't have lost much value in the two months. In this situation, your heirs won't be saddled with debt if you die. The only expenses they'll incur is your cost of dying, which your net worth would likely cover. Term insurance is not something you need right away; however, you may want to start investing in a cash-value life insurance policy because at your age the premiums are low.

CLIFFSNOTES RESOURCE CENTER

The learning doesn't need to stop here. CliffsNotes Resource Center shows you the best of the best — excellent resources to help you get more information about life insurance. I've included some books on related topics, Web sites that can help you do in-depth research on life insurance and get online quotes, and information about the five major independent ratings companies that judge insurance companies. And don't think that this is all we've prepared for you; we've put all kinds of pertinent information at **www.cliffsnotes.com**. Look for all these great resources at your favorite bookstore or local library and on the Internet. When you're online, make your first stop **www.cliffsnotes.com**, where you'll find more incredibly useful information about life insurance.

Books

If you're ready to move on to the next step, check out some of these other titles.

Personal Finance For Dummies, by Eric Tyson, helps you extend the learning experience into other areas of your financial life. IDG Books Worldwide, Inc. ISBN 0-7645-5013-6, published 1997. $19.99.

Consumer Reports Life Insurance Handbook by Jersey Gilbert, Ellen Schultz, and the editors of Consumer Reports Books. Consumer Reports Books. ISBN 0-8904-3708-4, published 1994. $16.95.

Your Life Insurance Options by Alan Lavine. Wiley. ISBN 0-4715-4919-3, published 1993. $12.95 (paper).

You can find these books in your favorite bookstores (on the Internet and at a store near you). We also have three Web sites that you can use to find out about all the books published by IDG Books Worldwide, Inc.:

- **www.cliffsnotes.com**
- **www.dummies.com**
- **www.idgbooks.com**

Internet

Some of the largest companies' Web sites offer good information about life insurance and their other products, calculators to help you determine the amount of coverage you need, and/or online quotes. Find company Web site addresses in ads, by calling a local agent, or just guess — type in www., fill in the name of the company, and then add .com. Check out these Web sites for more information about life insurance.

Life-Line, at **www.life-line.org**, gives an excellent introduction to life insurance, provides a calculator to help you determine how much insurance you need, and another one to help you determine your "value."

Insurance Online at InsWeb (**http://insweb.com**) offers basic information, a calculator, and instant quotes (based on limited information from you; actual premiums may vary) on term insurance from major insurance companies. This Web site is an excellent means to compare available prices with the price you get from an agent.

The Consumer Insurance Guide at **www.insure.com/life** provides tips, in-depth stories, and guidance on auto, homeowners, health, life, and business insurance, plus annuities.

SafeTnet.com, at **www.safetnet.com**, offers in-depth information about insurance and does extensive research about other Web sites. The folks behind SafeTnet.com visit and objectively review a huge number of Web sites that provide advice or insurance products to consumers.

Next time you're on the Internet, don't forget to drop by **www.cliffsnotes.com**. We created an online Resource Center that you can use today, tomorrow, and beyond.

Resource Kit

In this section, I include some organizations that you may find helpful as you navigate the realm of life insurance.

The National Association of Life Underwriters (NALU), 1922 F Street NW, Washington, DC 20006; phone 202-331-6000; Web site **http://nalu.org**.

Society of Financial Service Professionals, 270 S. Bryn Mawr Avenue, Bryn Mawr, PA 19010-2195; phone 610-526-2500; fax 610-527-4010.

The following five independent insurance company ratings organizations rate over 3,000 insurance companies to help you evaluate which one you should select. When considering any insurance company, check its rating from at least two ratings companies.

A.M. Best Company, Inc., Ambest Road, Oldwick, NJ 08858; phone 908-439-2200. This company doesn't have a Web site, but its ratings are available in libraries.

Duff & Phelps Credit Rating, 311 South Wacker Dr., Chicago, IL 60603; phone 312-697-4600 or 312-368-3198 (Ratings Hotline); Web site **www.dcrco.com**. Insurance company ratings are available online using a search engine.

Moody's Investors Service, 99 Church St., New York, NY 10007; phone 212-553-0300; Web site **www.moodys.com**; Individual insurance company ratings, listed alphabetically, are available on this Web site.

Standard & Poor's, 25 Broadway, 15th Floor, New York, NY 10004; phone 212-438-7200; Web site **www.standardand-poors.com/ratings/insurance/index.htm**. Individual insurance company ratings aren't easily uncovered online, but they are available in hardcopy in libraries.

Weiss Ratings, 4176 Burns Rd., Palm Beach Gardens, FL 33410; phone 561-627-3300, fax 561-625-668; Web site **www.weissratings.com**. Ratings aren't easily accessed online, but hardcopies are available in libraries.

Send Us Your Favorite Tips

In your quest for learning, have you ever experienced that sublime moment when you figure out a trick that saves time or trouble? Perhaps you realized you were taking ten steps to accomplish something that could have taken two. Or you've found a little-known workaround that gets great results. If you've discovered a useful tip that helped you navigate the maze of life insurance more effectively and you'd like to share it, the CliffsNotes staff would love to hear from you. Go to our Web site at **www.cliffsnotes.com** and click the Talk to Us button. If we select your tip, we may publish it as part of *CliffsNotes Daily,* our exciting, free e-mail newsletter. To find out more or to subscribe to a newsletter, go to **www. cliffsnotes.com** on the Web.

INDEX

COMING SOON FROM CLIFFSNOTES

Online Shopping

HTML

Choosing a PC

Beginning Programming

Careers

Windows 98 Home Networking

eBay Online Auctions

PC Upgrade and Repair

Business

Microsoft Word 2000

Microsoft PowerPoint 2000

Finance

Microsoft Outlook 2000

Digital Photography

Palm Computing

Investing

Windows 2000

Online Research

IDG BOOKS WORLDWIDE

COMING SOON FROM CLIFFSNOTES
Buying and Selling on eBay

Have you ever experienced the thrill of finding an incredible bargain at a specialty store or been amazed at what people are willing to pay for things that you might toss in the garbage? If so, then you'll want to learn about eBay — the hottest auction site on the Internet. And CliffsNotes *Buying and Selling on eBay* is the shortest distance to eBay proficiency. You'll learn how to:

- Find what you're looking for, from antique toys to classic cars

- Watch the auctions strategically and place bids at the right time

- Sell items online at the eBay site

- Make the items you sell attractive to prospective bidders

- Protect yourself from fraud

Here's an example of how the step-by-step CliffsNotes learning process simplifies placing a bid at eBay:

1. Scroll to the Web page form that is located at the bottom of the page on which the auction item itself is presented.

2. Enter your registered eBay username and password and enter the amount you want to bid. A Web page appears that lets you review your bid before you actually submit it to eBay. After you're satisfied with your bid, click the Place Bid button.

3. Click the Back button on your browser until you return to the auction listing page. Then choose View⇨Reload (Netscape Navigator) or View⇨Refresh (Microsoft Internet Explorer) to reload the Web page information. Your new high bid appears on the Web page, and your name appears as the high bidder.